Ecstasy

By
Bridget O. Juwah

For permission requests, write to the publisher, addressed "Attention:
Permissions Coordinator" at the email address below:

Life and Success Media Ltd

e-mail: info@abookinsideyou.com

www.lifeandsuccesspublishing.com

ISBN Number: 978-1-64764-509-0

Cover Design: Allan Sealy

Dedicated

TO

Austin Oghide and his lovely wife.

.

Content

Foreword

Ecstasy is a must read book for its many benefits to the body and soul. The romantic sparkles in relationships that this book discusses continually ignite endorphins and oxytocin toward sustaining emotional bliss in the lives of couples and partners. These romantic sparkles galvanize and electrify pertinent brain pleasure centers and formulate ribbons and roses with the ultimate goal of keeping marriages and relationships juicy for a life time.

Dr. Francis Linson
New York, USA.

Preface

The book "Ecstasy" is pleasurable and exciting, sizzling and entrancing.

Dr. Lawanda Bryant
California, USA.

Acknowledgement

Thanks to all who will read this book.

Scope - Health Foundation

The "Guns for Flowers" Program is aimed at reducing crime, suicide, and homicide all over the world.

Food, Water, and Medicine Program is an outreach Program meant to reach out to disaster victims and refugees in war torn countries of the world.

Advocacy Program is for greater government concern for vagrant psychotics to reduce social malaise and social menace.

Free Caesarean Sections for impoverished pregnant women to reduce the unacceptable rate of maternal mortality, especially in third world countries.

Sexuality Education Program to reduce incidences of abortion and baby dumping.

— Dr. Bridget O. Juwah
President, Health Foundation
healthfound@yahoo.com

About The Author

B ridget holds a Doctorate in Educational Leadership, and is a Professor of the Social Sciences. She conducted a multidisciplinary research in the fields of Sociology, Psychology and Medicine to produce this book. She is the Author of Flames of Love, Growing Up, and Where Angels Fear to Tread – The Skid Row Experiences. She was formerly the Head of Administration, Delta Steel Company Lagos, Nigeria, and now lives in California, USA.

Bridget is the President of Health Foundation Nigeria and USA. Health Foundation gives free medical aid to pregnant women and vagrant psychotics, organizes public lectures, symposia and television talk shows on socio-medical issues for societal development.

Bridget was an Independent Producer/Presenter of a popular Television Program "Talking Health" which she used as a medium to disseminate information on issues of drug abuse and reproductive health.

In Nigeria, through advocacy programs, Bridget brought government attention to the plight of the underprivileged. In the United States, she came face to face with a multi-racial multitude that hibernate in the downtown area of Los Angeles, California. Her exploits in this regard are documented in her book Where Angels Fear to Tread – The Skid Row Experiences.

SITTING IS PROF. F. GIWA OSAGIE, CONSULTANT IN OBSTETRICS AND GYNAECOLOGY, AND PROF. MRS. OGEDENGBE, CONSULTANT IN OBSTETRICS AND GYNAECOLOGY AT THE PUBLIC LECTURE ORGANIZED BY HEALTH FOUNDATION IN COLLABORATION WITH THE UNITED BANK FOR AFRICA IN JUNE 2002 AT THE BANKERS HOUSE, VICTORIA ISLAND, LAGOS.

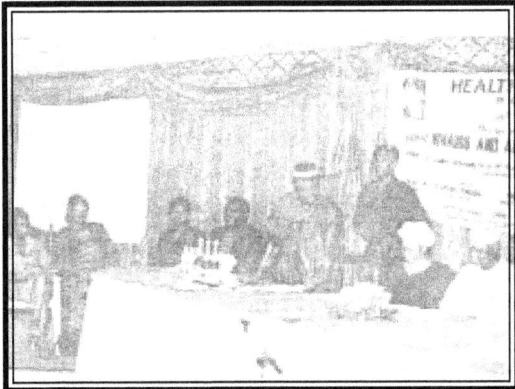

SECOND TO THE RIGHT IS THE FORMER FIRST LADY OF LAGOS STATE NIGERIA, MRS. OLUREMI TINUBU (SPECIAL GUEST OF HONOR) AT THE PUBLIC LECTURE, NEXT TO HER IS DR. LEKE PITAN (HON. COMMISSIONER FOR HEALTH IN LAGOS STATE) HOLDING THE MICROPHONE, GIVING HIS WELCOME ADDRESS AS CHAIRMAN OF THE OCCASION.

A PUBLIC LECTURE ORGANIZED BY THE HEALTH FOUNDATION IN
COLLABORATION WITH UNITED BANK FOR AFRICA ON 14 DECEMBER 2001
AT THE LAGOS TELEVISION HALL ON HIV/AIDS AND ABORTION AMONG
ADOLESCENTS.

A NEGLECTED WOMAN WHO DELIVERED HER BABY AT TANDLE
HOSPITALS, SURULERE, LAGOS (ANTE-NATAL AND DELIVERY EXPENSES
BORNE BY HEALTH FOUNDATION).

A NURSE IMMUNIZING THE BABY OF AN ABANDONED WOMAN AT THE RANSOME KUTI HEALTH CENTRE, LAGOS MS. BRIDGET JUWAH, PRESIDENT (HF) IN THE MIDDLE. HEALTH FOUNDATION PAID THE HOSPITAL BILLS.

MS. BRIDGET JUWAH (PRESIDENT) IN THE MIDDLE, MR. A. WYMAN—A BRITISH COUNTERPART AND MR. O. OLOJEDE—A MEMBER OF THE BOARD OF TRUSTEES (HF)

A HUSBAND WHO ABANDONED HIS WIFE IN PREGNANCY JOINS HER AFTER
SAFE DELIVERY WHICH WAS SPONSORED BY HF AT HARVEY HEALTH CENTRE
YABA, LAGOS.

MS. BRIDGET JUWAH (PRESIDENT) HF GIVING A GIFT AFTER A CLINICAL CHECK
UP AT PSYCHIATRIC HOSPITAL, YABA, LAGOS.

MS. BRIDGET JUWAH (PRESIDENT) HF RECEIVING A BABY BOY FROM HER
MOTHER DURING A VISIT TO THE RANDLE HEALTH CENTER, LAGOS. THE
WOMAN WAS ABANDONED AFTER BEING PUT IN THE FAMILY WAY AND WAS
ASSISTED BY THE FOUNDATION.

Ms. Bridget Juwah cutting the tape on the
Ground Breaking Ceremony of Health Foundation, USA.

Introduction

The book Ecstasy has delightful information for partners who need to give themselves quality pleasure. This will sustain libido and a high romantic impetus in relationships for a life time.

Couples delightfully will visit a romantic bed each night if they treat each other right. This will reduce the search for sexual variety and incidences of relationship break-ups.

Written in simple language, Bridget has emphasized that thrills and ecstatic moments are part of a whole romantic scene for marriages and long-term relationships.

⤝

1

The Bright Lights
Of Hollywood

Love lights up the whole sky

Hollywood, an exotic community of movie stars and film makers, where flourishing movie studios and tantalizing street lights adorn, is the relaxation spot of Nancy and Robert. They hibernate at this luscious city at the weekends to keep their love lives happy and frisky, and to rejuvenate their wedding vows. They go there to spoon under the bright stars and lights of the famous city.

Hollywood, known for motion picture productions and seductive living is the place where Robert and his wife of five years visit regularly to rekindle the ecstatic moments of their first meeting.

Nancy is a pretty brunette and a fashion icon with whom Robert became enamored. A sexy Italian high fashion model, with a stunning bone structure, Nancy is a rare combination of cute and sexy. She always wears sleek, sexy blond locks and is Robert's affectionate concern. Robert has the polish and suavity of a socialite and is Nancy's heartthrob. They share a profoundly tender feeling for each other and a feeling of warm personal attachment. They are a sweet couple, skilled in giving and receiving pleasure.

Serene Parks and Waterfalls and a bland southern breeze are features of the luscious city. There is a beehive of activities and trendy faces that grace the malls, cinemas, and other tourist attractions at the movie production capital. Hollywood is the world-famous center for film industry, and a haven for stars who want to make billboard history. The city provides stunning nightlife under the stars as well as glamorous poolside parties under the sun. On the steep hillsides of this boom town is Sunset Hotels and Resorts where Robert and Nancy visit for the cool evening breeze, and to ignite the romantic sparkle again. Basking under the bright lights of Hollywood is a perfect way to rev-up their evenings. They make "alone time" a priority, and they commit at least an evening every week to be alone.

Sunset Hotels is the secret retreat of Hollywood legends. Robert and Nancy plan erotic get-a-away and happy-hour weeknights in Hollywood to relax, refresh and recreate; because any arousing activity can trigger feelings of romance. They also re-invent their date nights with new and rejuvenating ideas; like walking holding hands under the attractive lights on the streets of Hollywood. Loving is intoxicating and for Robert and Nancy, moments of physical contact vastly strengthen their love. Sunset Hotels is one of their favorite romantic memories where Robert popped the question to Nancy. They get cozy hanging out there under the low lit chandeliers as a sexy new couple. This helps them to re-live the ecstasy of that moment when Nancy's eyes dilated at the sight of a blue sapphire engagement ring. It was a mesmerizing delight as Robert went down on his knees to ask Nancy to marry him. Sunset Hotel is also a place where couples could share quiet peace, and it brings nostalgic memories as well.

Nancy is an astonishing model who wears clingy clothes that emphasize her flattering figure. Her svelte physique and exquisite fashion always make Robert's eyes spark with ravishing delight. She is a fashion icon, a radiant personality with an impeccable sense of style. She makes sexual and sensual color choices of clothes, and wears high definition eyelashes with bold eye shades. They like keeping their relationship thrilling and sexy; to entertain themselves and avert matrimonial boredom. Marriage is like a garden that needs to be nourished and nurtured. Unsavory and sordid conditions could stifle the one-time romantic union.

From the Sunset Hotels and Resorts, Nancy and Robert could overlook Beverly Hills, one of the most affluent cities in the world, and the home of Hollywood celebrities. While at the Sunset Hotels, they would treat themselves to romantic dinners and champagne cocktails in the dimly lit and cozy restaurant. Sometimes, they would have different types of exotic foods and assorted wines for the most refreshing get-a-way. With instrumental jazzy music filtering through the atmosphere, the ideal atmosphere for lovers is created. The couple would relax through the evening, watching a galaxy of music performers and exotic dancers at the hotel basement.

Nancy always would recline on Robert's shoulders for that assuring feeling that she is loved and appreciated. Robert, in reciprocation would run his fingers occasionally through her hair, and that sent pleasurable sensations through her spine. This pleasurable act causes their bodies to release a flood of feel-good chemicals that trigger specific physical reactions. Robert gave Nancy assurances of his love and appreciation in affectionate whispering tones to assure his damsel that she is his charming delight because lovers should pay compliments to each other often. The glitzy environment always brought elation to their demeanor, and they found the weekend evening outings a good recreation, and revitalization of their wedding vows to love and to cherish each other forever.

They would take to the dancing floor to remind themselves of how it was in the very beginning. Dance and eyes' dancing are non-verbal forms of communications; even bees have been known to dance to attract their partners. Dance is healthy for the body. It is also a recipe for weight reduction and a medically recommended form of in-door and out-door exercises. Robert and Nancy entertained themselves with different dance steps as reminders of their first date when Robert was elated with the "capture" of his damsel. They attended occasions for celebrity showcasing, dance songs, and ballads as normal routine. Robert enjoyed seeing Nancy express herself again with her gyrations on the dance floor, for that youthful nostalgic feeling. In feeling and looking youthful, you are sending messages to the brain that you are not aged yet and that you are still relevant in the scheme of things. This has potentials to slow the aging process and stimulate a more bubbling you.

Nancy loved the shrimp cocktails with little shots of white wine. She loved Italian meals with the finest Italian flavors. She usually would have veal scaloppini with saffron cream sauce whereas Robert would have chicken vesuvio and rigatoni with steak sauce. Eating out at the weekends is exhilarating to couples; it is always an exciting event to look forward to and a break from normal routine.

It was a cool summer evening and Robert and Nancy decided to catch a glimpse of the bright lights of Hollywood. Nancy was wearing a form fitting black skirt accented by Christian Louboutin black heels. This emphasized her luscious figure and her earrings were custom-made Fred

Leighton diamond chandelier danglers. The couple made their way to the movie theaters to watch some motion pictures. They went to celebrate the opening of the season's romantic movie event. It was another charming evening at the Grove Movie Theaters for Nancy and Robert. They would choose different scenarios each weekend; for purposes of variety and to add pep to their matrimonial lives. It was either frolicking on the beach or taking a walk down the beautifully lit streets of Hollywood for that experience that light up their fantasies. They are a really sweet couple who are resolved to create moments of ecstasy.

Hand-in-hand, Robert and Nancy would make their entrance into the theater, and locate a suitable sit at the rear. Holding hands is an enigmatic body language that signifies a powerful bonding and understanding between lovers and married persons. It strikes a concordance tune as lovers walk hand-in-hand in voluntary accord. It suggests ownership of your sweetheart, and it is a positive affirmation of a loving relationship. Couples that are mentally divorced do not hold hands because things have fallen apart. It was a romantic/comedy adult film. They cuddled and had fun that brought the twinkle again to their eyes. It was the most romantic and endearing evening. It was love in Hollywood where the glitz and the glamour made for relaxation, and good sightseeing.

They usually would drive through the brightly lit streets of this celebrity community at summer time with their convertible Mercedes Sports to allow the cool evening breeze refresh their frayed nerves from a hectic work week. The bright lights of Hollywood excite Nancy and Robert tremendously because the scenery adds color to their romantic union. It gives them the opportunity to hurdle together in youthful exuberance and to maintain a satisfying sex life as a couple.

It was summery weather in July when Robert and Nancy had another romantic night-out in Hollywood. Nancy with an exotic hair style was unquestionably fabulous in a purple frock featuring cut-outs at the waist. They were at Ross Hotels to entertain themselves with champaign cocktails in celebration of their fifth wedding anniversary. They were determined to have a fun-filled and memorable celebration. It was an exciting evening, and a sweet bonding for the love birds. As they arrived to their posh home in West Los Angeles, it was a revitalized and smiling pair; ready for the midnight ecstasy.

When two people are attracted to each other, a virtual frenzy of hormone and neurochemical activity occurs. By increasing desire and arousal, there is also enhanced bonding between the partners. As Nancy and Robert sank into their Jacuzzi for that freshness from the soapy water bubbles, it was another moment of physical contact for the two love birds. Getting ready for a captivating evening, Nancy wore a sweet smelling talc powder with an easy access nightgown for a pleasurable time with her hussy in their ultra-romantic bedroom. A romantic bed is always a happy bed to visit each night. Robert is her best friend whom she cuddles and loves for every chance she gets.

Concluding the evening with bluesy music and cool lights in their bedroom, electrifying sensations swept through their brain pleasure centers, which ignited high libido. Romance is the real deal that keeps a relationship juicy. Romance is a frenzy of wild and intoxicating feeling, much needed by couples for thrilling moments. Robert and Nancy are also a musical couple, for they always allow the music talk the talk for them and lead them into their utopic world. They attained ecstatic heights as they soared via the music "airbus" along with cupid into galaxies unknown; heights of rapturous delight where they communicate with whispers of love and appreciation for who they are. It was quality time on bed for the twosome as their excitement boost oxytocin, which is the bonding hormone released during new, exciting activities that bring together.

Oxytocin is released during orgasm and intense emotional states. Orgasm is the ultimate human sexual pleasure as endorphins soak the brain, and one is immersed in intense pleasurable sensations. Orgasms add 8-10 extra years to the human life span, and it plays a crucial role in the longevity of a relationship. It was therefore, sweet slumber, and intriguing dreams for Nancy and Robert on that memorable night. They woke up at dawn mesmerized with a sense of pleasure, happy with romantic rejuvenation of being with each other; as they look forward to another weekend of bliss, and the bright lights of Hollywood.

2

Winter Romance In The Skies

My electrifying radiance!

It was a beautiful summer evening, and Ted flashed a flirty smile at Michelle whom he met at the Casey Cocktail Bar. Ted delightfully requested Michelle to join him for a drink. Michelle was in a plum Isaac Mizrahi and her signature pearls looked ravishing, and she had an impeccable sense of style. Michelle astounded, and speechless, had a fixed gaze at Ted. Confounded by his optimism, Michelle shrugged her shoulders, gave a polite smile and retracted from Ted's invitation. She bade the stranger goodbye and took quick steps to the exit door of the Bar. Hopping into her Lexus convertible, she heaved a sigh of relief as she drove away.

A week later, Michelle pulled up at the parking lot of a Mall to have a sauna bath, facials, and a massage. She was getting ready for face modeling that she hoped would push her into the spotlight in her career. As she stepped out elegantly, there was Ted wearing sunglasses and a piquant designer T-shirt on brown jeans. Apparently, he was getting into the Mall to have a haircut. Michelle, wearing a lacy bandeau top and see-through crocheted white skirt and high heeled white shoes, gave a surprise smile to Ted whose pupils dilated with ravishing delight and expectancy.

Ted became breathless at the sight of Michelle because he had longed to meet her again. He requested Michelle to join him at the VIP Lounge for a chat. Michelle tendered an apology to the painstaking and resilient Ted because she was on a very tight schedule. Michelle, however, requested for Ted's business card promising to get back with him. Ted, handing over his business card to Michelle wished that she would give him a quick call.

As days went by, Ted waited anxiously for a surprise call. He however, maintained a cautious optimism as he looked forward to the call of a life time. He had only a little sleep each night as thoughts of Michelle consumed him. Ted would gaze into space acting out sexual fantasies of his bewitching gazelle.

It was a cold winter afternoon and three months after Michelle had met Ted at the Mall. Michelle arrived at the VIP lounge at the Mall, and she saw Ted sipping a drink. Michelle sat comfortably and relaxed on a sofa in the lounge. The lounge was warm and toasty and Ted made some hurried steps toward Michelle. Ted with renewed enthusiasm hoped that cupid would give him a good day with the blonde. The stormy whether had caused Michelle to retreat into the VIP Lounge for a hot drink. The waiter approached Michelle, and she requested for a steaming cup of coffee with chocolate cream and meat burgers.

Handing Michelle the Essence Magazine, Ted informed her that he runs a publishing company for soft selling magazines that feature models, fashions and top-of –the-line automobiles. Michelle retorted "I am top-of-the-line model and I have exquisite and entrancing photos that you can publish." Ted interjected "it will be simply delightful to have a peep into your world of high fashion modeling and see the energy, the pop, the tension, and charisma that you bring into the industry. When I peruse your photos, I will be able to advice on the new dimensions about the run-way walk and more elegant poise and postures." Ted continued "I recruit models and do photo shoots that could feature in tabloid press as well. I train on how you can re-invent yourself, to know more of the angles of your body and how you can play with your proportions." Michelle is cute with flattering angles and a perfect sculptic face. With a stoic elegance and poise, she has a top model potential. Michelle has a stunning bone structure and a strong walk; that gives that signature move on the run way.

Michelle, in sleek, natural-looking faux-hair pieces to get beautiful looking effects and wearing a clingy red dress with a dainty fur coat suitable for the winter season, accepted Ted's invitation to visit his office. She paid a curtsey call at his office three days later. Ted was pleasantly surprised at the august visitor. He was also very well groomed, looking clean, crisp, and rich. Ted has a posh office that overlooks a rose garden. There were olive green drapes on his office windows and a dainty glass executive desk. Hanging on the walls were astonishing and gorgeous pictures of fitness and fashion models, including sexy super models.

It was the end of a business day, and Ted and Michelle were sipping hot coffee laced with chocolate mix in the cozy office that overlooked the well groomed rose gardens. As they stepped into the exterior, was the studio for the great photo shoots, and there were also make-up artists. In a short while, Michelle had a make-over and was shining in a Calvin Klein and dress ensemble. That was a new look that highlighted her body proportions. She was ready to use the set to her advantage and project herself as a high fashion professional model.

Michelle switched outfits to a retro-looking gold gown with elbow-length gloves and popped a gorgeous pose. Another photo pose was Michelle wearing a pale blue, shimmering Azzedine Alaia gown and Rapunzel-length weaves. Another pose was Michelle in chic black ensemble with trendy sleeves and matching pumps that highlighted her signature curves. She also had on the most iconic dress, which could make waves on the front pages of the magazines. She popped a pose in a jarring jump suit and tricked the camera, playing with her exotic body angles; she would inhale, whenever the camera goes up. She had good size boobs and a sparkly sex appeal. She exuded tension, force, and professionalism as much as the more sexualized celebs and runway models. Michelle qualified to appear on countless Choice Girl Magazine covers for developing a great body, and a special face for face modeling.

Michelle was scheduled to take part in an international fashion show in Paris a month later. Ted and his make-up artists were abreast with the great challenge to showcase the peculiar and exquisite qualities of Michelle. Michelle has a runway passion, and she practically performs as if she owned the runway. At the international fashion show, she turned heads in a chic Alexander McQueen frock and massive McQueen belt, and a black platform peep-toe that completed her flawless looks. She later switched apparels and made a buzzing appearance in a glittering garment with a plunging neckline that also showcased her unique assets.

She excelled in back turns in such a way that make eye shadows pop. The fashion blogs were earnestly abuzz with just how to get Michelle's "snooki" Polizzi's hairstyle. She was a rare combination of beauty, elegance and style. She stood out as a model of indefinable origin to the great delight of Ted who had flash backs of their first meeting. The paparazzi were all over her as they stumbled on each other to get sensuous shots of a high fashion model. Michelle was awarded the first position. She stood out in a curve-hugging red and black frock at the awards show.

The fashion show was a complete success, and Michelle watched the electronic and print media glamorize her shots. With so much of media frenzy around her, she was clearly a star set to make billboard history. Her rise to superstardom has been meteoric, and it is obvious that her outstanding performance will give her global publicity and a good fan base. Ted, feeling elated at the exciting contest proposed a dinner date to Michelle to celebrate the astounding success. Michelle delightfully accepted the date and Ted was getting hopelessly hooked on Michelle. They made their way to the Moonlight Hotels and Resorts for a historic get-together. It was a splendid evening as they wined and dined, watching a galaxy of opera singers. Michelle, wearing a blue fitted satin gown with a tiny waist and sculpted arms beamed with radiant smiles all through the evening. It was a winter dinner, blissful, and memorable. Michelle had struck the deal of a life time that was worthy of celebration. The success will push her into the spotlight and the realization of her dream world as Cover Girl for a magazine known for glamour and pageantry.

It was a spectacular evening as they treated themselves with appetizing delicacies and exotic Italian wines. That was a great "alone time" for Ted and Michelle. They had eye-to-eye communication that is affected by the love hormone oxytocin; critical for intimate emotional communication. It was sweet bonding between Ted and Michelle as their conversation began to reflect a sense of togetherness. Stepping out of the Moonlight Hotels, they looked an exquisite twosome as they held hands in one accord; hopeful for exciting careers and the most romantic life together. The thrills of the trip, and the thrilling evening was most entrancing and their hearts danced in their orbits in a brief romantic glimpse of the future.

It was time to say goodbye to Paris. The elegant and colorful model arrived at the airport in a dress that revealed her midriff and an exotic hairstyle. They sat together in the first class cabin of the Boeing 747 that flew them from Paris to New York. It was a long night flight, and in the dim lights of the plane, Ted whispered to Michelle "you are my heartthrob; it's been sweet feelings." Something about a whisper in the ear is a huge turn-on.

They both developed a profound physical and emotional need for touch. Vasopressin is directly released through touch into the brain where it facilitates bonding and social behavior. Michelle was quiet and sought for his biceps to lay her head in silent consent. His biceps twitched with delight for the sweet feeling and in masculine expression of a welcome to his long sought "dream," he clasped his arms around her. As they were entering into a state of love, they were "floating" in the skies almost immune from the worries of the world. It was winter romance in the skies! They were many miles above the sea level, and they were greeted occasionally by the turbulent winds. The cold air within the airplane enveloped them, and their bodies disseminated the warmth that spoke even in their muteness. They remained silent and breathless and basked in that warmth until the flight hostess interrupted their "new world" with the midnight snacks. Falling in love causes the body to release certain chemicals that trigger specific physical reactions.

As they refreshed themselves, Ted gave Michelle a sip of his hot brewed coffee and Michelle fed Ted with her cookies. It was a magical evening and a moment of love. It was a sizzling romance in the skies! Romance is as inexplicable as the beauty of the rainbow and love lightens up the pleasure centers of the brain. It was an exhilarating feeling, and once again Michelle sought for Ted's biceps for a warm repose in the cool of the flying bird propelled by high-tech engines. Ted responded by tilting his shoulders to support his new love for the sweet sleep of life. Ted from time to time ran his hands through her blond hair and soft body. The experience of falling in love comes with a unique blend of energy and exhilaration that result in a near euphoric state. It was a stunning experience. It was cock crow at dawn as the Boeing 747 touched the tarmac at the Kennedy International Airport in New York.

As Ted and Michelle alighted from the plane, they sat for a while at the VIP lounge of the International Airport to have a flighty breakfast. They shared identities for a few moments as they enveloped themselves in a hug at the lounge. They were to do dinner dancing at the weekend. They boarded the cab and exchanged kisses that will keep them reminiscing about each other until their next meeting.

Ted presented Michelle with sweet smelling flowers at their next meeting. A dating spree began which captivated Ted, and he was determined to make a marriage proposal to Michelle. Ted invited her for another night out which was the defining moment for the couple.

All bubbles, dressed in an eclectic outfit that included an embellished leather jacket, trendy tights and dreamy earrings, Michelle arrived for the unique date. It was an eye-catching ensemble. Ted, in a high collar shirt and a tuxedo suit with a touch of the Givenchi collections was waiting for Michelle at the lounge. They watched a galaxy of opera stars, and blues singers and they did the gig on the dance floor as well. After mild gyrations, they retired to the rear of the lounge, which had soft dim chandeliers hanging from the roof tops. Ted whispered to Michelle "you blow my mind; will you be my girl?" Michelle seemed to suggest with dreamy eyes "your wife." Through the pupils of her eyes, and underneath the well layered eye shadows, Ted perceived her answers.

As Ted held her with great passion, as he inhale the timeless perfumes all over her tantalizing body, he buried his head in her bosom and gave a sigh of relief. Her heart buzzed with delight as Ted slipped a 6.1-carat pink diamond engagement ring into her well-manicured fingers. That was a perfect way to rev-up their evening and their hearts seemed to be humming along in harmony. It was a sweet evening, an evening to remember, an evening that their hearts tied the nuptial nuts in silence, an evening that their palpitating hearts prepared their wedding vows. It was clear that their roots were entwined together, and it was inconceivable that they would ever part.

They blended into a really sweet couple and as the spring season was budding its first flowers, Ted flew to the Canary Islands to give his heart to his "angel." They became engulfed in a post wedding bliss and toured the island in rapturous delight. Far away in the Canaries, they discovered the mystery of the "honey" dripping from the "moon" and their hearts sang along with the singing birds.

⌒

3

It's Freezing Cold

Best romantic moments

It was freezing cold on a winter evening when the icy wind from the famous beaches in New York blew snowy flakes all around Andy and Diane. They were in a close hug shivering in their winter coats. They became glued to themselves in sweet bonding, receiving warmth from each other in the freezing cold. The chill of the evening dictated their romantic posture as they shivered and shriveled into each others arms. Their chemistry was at a high blend and Andy enveloped Diane with his coat, and adjusted her mufflers in the freezing cold. The loving act brought warmth to Diane's numb fingers who reciprocated by hugging Andy at the nape of his neck. Hugging situates lovers in a touching position, which provides a physical stimulus.

There was a sudden drizzle in the freezing cold that made Andy pull his umbrella over Diane, and she shriveled into his body clinging onto his biceps with desperation. The cold weather exhilarated them, and they clung to each other pleasurably. They had dated for three years; profusely in love with each other, and they looked forward to a romantic evening in the midst of the icy weather. Their eyes dazzled with expectation of ecstatic moments on this winter evening. It was the beginning of the month and up in the sky was the new moon beaming faint light rays in the midst of dark and eerie clouds. Diane was shining in a Calvin Klein coat and dress ensemble suitable for a winter night out. Hurdled underneath the umbrella with his heartthrob, Andy felt good with her unique fragrance and soft feel.

Diane is an astounding, and gorgeous make-up artist. She was wearing a sleek, sexy, and straight hair style. She had a touch of blush to give her face some color. She has great looks, an arresting figure, and a faultless sense of fashion. A quintessential society girl, Diane emits a personality that is admired and revered. Andy on his part grew a distinctive moustache with well-trimmed side burns. He was wearing exquisite blazers for the evening; smelling good and looking good. He had a flattering diamond engagement ring tucked away in his inner pocket; for he had planned to give Diane a piquant surprise. He had arranged a romantic place for proposing to his hearthrob.

Diane had a romantic dinner with Andy a fortnight prior. It was birthday celebrations for Andy and Diane gave him a sumptuous candle light dinner at the Ritzy Restaurant. It was an exquisite place known for its beautiful layout on top of the mountains overlooking the Mediterranean. Stepping inside the hotel lobby was a set of brightly lit chandeliers which made a gracious lighting impression on the twosome. They made their way to the Restaurant section for some delicacies. Special treats like champaign, chocolates, strawberries, candle light dinners and warm nights at the fireplace can make an otherwise gloomy winter day seem oh-so-sweet. A little shot of red wine brought warmth to their faces as they were far away from the freezing cold and the raindrops. It was an elating environment with a good blend of jazz and classical music.

The unsuspecting Diane was once again at her best. She was perfectly coiffed and manicured and wearing the ideal shade of red lipstick. Her immaculate appearance is often a force to be reckoned with. At the entrance to the swanky hotel, the waiters took delivery of their winter coats for safe keeping. Diane looking appetizing with great size boobs and butt, and a signature slim frame, sat on a dimly lit table for two. Andy took a quick look again at Diane who stared at Andy with her penetrating and big eyeballs. She has "googley eyes" that twinkle with every little excitement. Eye-to-eye communication is critical to intimate emotional communication and the love hormone, oxytocin can be released in the body by a certain look with couples entering into a state of love. This flighty exchange brought a simmering delight to both of them as they were getting cozy. They sat together for that bi-directional flow of energy because it was freezing cold. In a demonstration of love, Andy ran his fingers through Diane's hair and that tickled her making her breathless for a brief moment. This is because oxytocin promotes bonding between a man and woman through touch.

It was a romantic evening and a candle light dinner for two gave them a unique "alone time." They started off with hot chicken soups and later settled for the main meal of lobsters and a choice range of sea foods. Andy wanted to give Diane her choice meal because Diane loves aquatic life and fishing is her hobby. Additionally, a meal of large red lobsters always make her eyes light up. It was a great evening for Andy because he was poised to make a marriage proposal to Diane on that freezing evening.

They cuddled, kissed intermittently, and cast loving glances at each other. After dinner, they relaxed at the Hotel's Penthouse located on the tenth floor of the hotel building. There, they watched ballads, dance songs, and blues inspired singers entertain the penthouse audience. With his hands wrapped around her waist, they were lost in each other's arms with the soothing bluesy music. Andy whispered loving words into her ears as they shriveled into themselves on the dimly lit dance floor. It was an ecstatic moment as the bluesy tunes took them to utopian heights causing their bodies to release the "love hormone" vasopressin.

Just before midnight, they made their way to the hotel suites to conclude the romantic date night. These are luxury ocean view suites with dimly lit chandeliers to kindle the romantic spirit. They took their time to inhale the sensual aromas in the suite. Slouching on a sofa in the comfortable hotel suite, and cuddling while sipping white wine, Andy proposed to his heartthrob with the sparkling Neil Lane ring. It was ruby red and offset by diamonds. It was their best romantic moment as Diane was speechless and teary-eyed. It was ecstasy as Diane glued her warm body to his warm chest, and shivered with unspeakable delight.

The hotel suite looked serene and had deep blue bedside lamps that created an alluring atmosphere for the love birds. The room was adorned with flowers that included several tropical exotics with showy bloom. It was a romantic bedroom, and the lighting made the room look sexy. Kissing her all over her body in the cozy bedroom, Andy asked if they could have a winter wedding. In the spirit of strong emotions and personal attachment, Andy promised to love and cherish her forever. They had a magical evening and a sweet bonding as a couple. They woke up at dawn mesmerized by the magical evening. Checking out from their hotel suite, Andy opened the door for his jewel, and they drove in their limousine in the freezing cold through the streets of New York.

It was an exciting experience as Diane and Andy had wedding planners set up the gorgeous wedding. They celebrated their upcoming nuptials with a rehearsal dinner. On the wedding day, Diane was wearing a georgette mermaid gown with hand-pieced Chantilly lace applique on the bodice. She wore a diamond headpiece for her veil, and her long brunette locks up in a bun. She was a vision in ivory. A celebrity audience graced the wedding on a cold winter morning. The snowflakes were falling gracefully to usher the bride and groom into the wedding chapel. Her wedding dress was sexy and untraditional. They shared passionate wedding vows and the best moments of their lives in the freezing cold.

4

Much Sex,
Little Romance

I searched for his biceps all night long;
biceps strong and firm.

Romance is the real deal that keeps a relationship juicy. Romance is the mystery associated with love. It provides the opportunity to rekindle the sensual spirit of a relationship. Romance also recaptures the essence of true love. There are many things that should fascinate us with our partners that could give us a "high" all day long.

Romance is the garden on which lovers sit. Nourishing a love relationship with romance, keeps it an ever-green garden. This is based on commitment, affection, and devotion. Affection, cuddles and romantic gestures are part of a whole romantic scene for lovers.

Couples tend to forget the importance of hugs when familiarity becomes part of their lives. Couples should not let the spark leave their unions and they should not fall out of love at the same time; someone got to sustain it. Romantic walks, visits to the pub, and the cinemas are essentials in a love relationship. Couples should spend a few romantic evenings in eating dinner by candlelight three times a month, engaging in a proper conversation six times a month and curling up in front of the TV together seven times a month at the least. Romantic weekends away from home are keys for a great relationship. Couples should snuggle together on a rainy day and wrap into one another while watching romantic movies. Couples should sometimes take a bubble bath together or slow dance to romantic music to entertain themselves and for that exhilarating feeling. Couples should take a walk down memory lane and visit some of the special places from early days of dating. A good marriage would also allow each partner to enjoy a night away from home without the other, in the company of their own friends.

Couples should look forward to romantic moments, and compulsorily make romantic overtures to each other everyday to spice their romantic lives. Romantic overtures season the day, and a couple is set for the utmost expression of love. Romance tickles the brain pleasure centers and transmits the vibrations down the spine to the parts of the body, thus preparing the body for anecdotal experiences and ecstatic heights. Romance should be the highlight of a relationship because it emphasizes quality foreplay and not rigorous sex or the number of "rounds" a man can give a woman. Couples should get cozy and sassy at every opportunity to keep their relationship juicy and frisky. Small acts of physical intimacy – the hand on the small of the back as you brush by in the hallway, your arm around their shoulder on the sofa, your hand on their thigh when seated side-by-side, holding hands while walking down the street – give your partner a warm feeling and convey the love and affection you feel for them. Lovers should plan occasional trips to beaches; because beaches are the paradise for lovers.

Romance is fixing something or the house just to make your partner happy. Romance is grooming yourself to look good for your partner and doing some sexy role-playing. Express your love in a different way to your partner every day, and occasionally declare your love publicly to your partner. It brings reassuring comfort into the relationship, and makes love making naturally sweet and smooth.

Convey your love with a radiant smile, and a direct soft eye contact and sometimes sing a favorite song into your lover's ears. Romance is a sizzling and refreshing feeling, and it excites the love hormones for that unifying act of pleasure. Romance is the "fertilizer" of a healthy relationship, and just like your garden, your relationship needs to be watered and fertilized regularly. Romance defies a timetable and should be spontaneous between couples to re-ignite the old flame. Romance will not happen until you make it happen. Cuddle on the sofa and watch a movie over a glass of juice or wine, and let there be the clinking of the wine glasses, which is a romantic music for lovers.

Relax in the arms of your partner and light two fragrance-scented candles at such spicy moments. Take your partner out to the movie or occasional candle light dinner for recreation and to rejuvenate the romantic cords. You could take a bubble bath together with your lover or greet your lover with a toasty warm towel as he or she steps out from the showers. Take your time to admire and to touch the details of your partner's body and introduce your fantasies to the bedroom; just observing your partner's body could arouse you for that ultimate pleasure.

Intimate touching makes a big difference in love making. If you make your partner's heart beat a little faster, yours will beat along with it, and romance can be as simple as saying "I love you." Lovers and married couples should capture the essence of romance in their lifelong relationship, and enjoy an expanding intimate connection. Romance is as inexplicable as the beauty of a rainbow, and romantic glances convey unspoken words of love. Couples should be musical and let their music choices do the talking for them. Lights and body language should suggest moods to couples and a little gift, an off-hand compliment, a moment of physical contact can vastly strengthen an emotional relationship.

There is a "chase" and a "capture" that precede relationships and lovers should not forget those initial acts that brought them together. The memories of the first meeting, the first embrace, the first kiss, and the closing of the eyes should remain indelible in the minds of lovers and married couples. Your partner's body statistics and the hunting scenario of the "chase" and the subsequent "capture" should be propellers that re-kindle the romantic spirit between couples. The ecstatic feelings of the "beginning" and the elating feeling of the first call or knock on the door should form the romantic foundations of a relationship. The spinal chills during the proposal, the fantasies of the wedding day, the first love making, and the first spark that ignited your fancy of your partner are among the many landmarks that should remain indelible in the minds of lovers. It is a colorful world to live in when lovers are in tacit accord with each other, and understand the body of their partner. Lovers should work toward "knowing" who their partners really are and how they want to be satisfied.

Some women who have undergone circumcision or female genital mutilation could experience low libido. Female circumcision is the partial or total cutting away of the external female genitalia. During the operation, all or part of the clitoris or labia are removed, and this can hinder sexual arousals in women; making the affected women to require more stimulation before sexual intercourse. These surgical procedures have no health benefits for girls and women. It is internationally recognized as a violation of the human rights of girls and women. It reflects deep rooted inequality between the sexes and constitutes an extreme of discrimination against women.

Sex should be introduced in the midst of heightened romantic pleasures when both partners (not only one) are ready for the sexual experience. Sex is where you go to be intimate and to love for that ecstatic and hypnotic feeling. Making love is a sexual activity that expresses the love, passion, and other strong feelings you have for another person. It is a beautiful emotional experience that can bring two people closer. Making love is giving yourself, body and soul over to your partner for ravishing delights. It is a time you and your partner both feel relaxed. It is a time of giving the best of you and a sexier you to the one you love. It is supposed to be a time to be under the soft lights and soothing music for more pleasurable and relaxing experience. Cool, soft lights are sensuous, and music is the song for the soul. They have mesmerizing effects and can prepare the mind and body for that intense expression of emotions to the one you love.

Love making is a concert of two hearts in a celebration of love. It is a privileged time to woo and entertain your partner again. Love making is a giving performance because it unlocks the doors, and gives access into the deepest recesses of the heart. Love making should make mental impressions that should be retained, and revived by the couple. Love making can bring forth a new life, kindle a new romantic spirit in couples and flame up the waning embers of love. It is a delightful experience when done with the right intensions.

Making love is holding your lover tightly clasped to your bosom and not letting go. It is that sweet struggle to catch another breath during your most elated moments. Love making is precious moments to remember, moments to cherish, moments to whisper your appreciation to your partner for another opportunity to express your emotions. Love making is an intense sensual relationship that brings two hearts in tacit concert; a concert of exploration of their bodies in an adventurous fashion.

Bedroom adventures to locate the most benign angles that could trigger the greatest excitement in your lover are necessary for the thrilling experience. Love making is not a hurried affair. It is a time to spend quality time with your sweet heart for most refreshing moments; moments that should be treasured for a life time. It is a time to let your partner know who you are and what your mean. It is a time to share warmth and intense affection in a romantic spirit. Love making is a time to forget past hurts, to cry on the shoulders of your partner, to let go and to submit to the passions of the heart.

It is a tender feeling when you drift into the realm of the sublime disconnected from planet earth for an orgasmic experience. Orgasm is the physical and emotional sensation experienced at the peak of sexual excitation, usually resulting from stimulation of the sexual organ and usually accompanied in the male by ejaculation of semen. Orgasm is a healthy experience, and it is an intense and unrestrained excitement. It is characterized by extremely pleasurable sensations. Constant orgasms have potentials to add 8-10 extra years to one's life span. It is a great recipe for good health and relationship longevity. The thrills of yesterday should have a natural lead to the thrills of the next day to ensure smooth continuity of romantic feelings. The thrills of yesterday should keep your partner looking forward for a sexier you and for more anecdotal experiences. Keeping your relationship romantic and sexy averts matrimonial boredom.

The environment for this expression of intense emotions contributes to the ecstatic feelings. A warm cozy bedroom for the winter season and a cool cozy bedroom in the hot summer season are conducive to coitus. An easy way to create romantic moods is to focus attention on lighting. Cool soft lights and the mood altering powers of sweet scented candlelight are essential for a romantic moment for couples. Couples should be musical and allow the music penetrate their soul and talk for them. This gives the couple sufficient stimulation time to emit the "love hormones" oxytocin and vasopressin. Quality romance is "juicy interactions," and it is an essential prelude to love making.

These romantic ingredients could be going out to your favorite romantic restaurant, watching a movie you both enjoy, giving each other a massage on your water bed or taking a warm Jacuzzi bubble bath together. Tease yourselves into the bedroom for those mind blowing experiences as you also discuss what you imagine doing to your bodies. The conversation will heighten the excitement. Easy access at-home clothes for couples aid intimacy, and it encourages spontaneity that keeps relationships springy.

Be super affectionate and respectful to your partner to keep your relationship entrancing. No matter how good your relationship with your partner is, there is room for a little bit more romance.

Women by their nature and make up need a longer time to get stimulated for sexual intercourse. Men on the other hand, are more easily aroused and ready for sexual experiences. Men should be selfless and give the woman more romantic impetus to be at the same romantic height before penetration. More time should, therefore, be given to romance and fore play to prepare the female body for sweet intercourse. This will cause more pleasure for the couple when the woman is ready for the act. Most of the time, women are given sex with very little romance, and this is entirely wrong and uneventful. Most men do not have a clue of how to pleasure women sexually.

A woman will keep coming back over and over begging for more if the man knows how to wow or mesmerize her body. The period of foreplay, including clitoral stimulation is the most important part of love making. Ideally, foreplay should be mutual sexual stimulation, and a necessary erotic prelude to sexual intercourse.

Some women attain orgasm during foreplay without vaginal intercourse. Foreplay defines the heights the couple will attain sexually. Sometimes, the men are in a hurry to gain penetration; sometimes they are just naïve, and do not realize how to pleasure the female body. Some women feel excruciating pain when the vagina is not well lubricated before penetration. This condition will hinder the couple from attaining orgasmic heights. Ideally, couples should have mind-blowing orgasms every time, and this naturally will enhance the desire for another sexual experience. It is worthy to mention that women get frustrated and lonely when men fall immediately asleep after an intense orgasm.

Violent sex and forceful penal thrusts may be averse to sexual pleasure for the woman. It may cause bruises or soreness in or around the vaginal region. Painful intercourse or inability to attain orgasm can make women avoid sex altogether. Unfortunately, some men have been socialized into believing that many rounds of sex and forceful penal thrusts determine their masculinity and sexual prowess. Paradoxically, some women suffer exhaustion with the thrusts because of excruciating pain. These women who resent forceful sex for reasons varied and individualized would rather prefer gentle and soothing thrusts to achieve orgasm and ecstatic heights.

Sometimes, women fake orgasms when they do not know how to make their man to stop when they are in pain. Faking orgasms incidentally can destroy relationships in the long term. Women sacrifice their sexual satisfaction just to save their men's ego, and they do not want to be labeled a slut or a whore. More than 85% of women do not experience sexual satisfaction, and they do not tell their men. Some women submit to the sexual advances of their men out of duty and not as mutual desire.

Sex means two different things to men and women. A male needs sexual release upper and foremost. This is just plain raw sex, and he doesn't care where it comes from. His body is pouring chemicals to his brain to cause a driving need for sexual release. This need is as real as his requirement for food, and his appetite. A man should meet the woman's expectation of long-time care and romance to get mutual appetite for sex. Most women cheat because of sexual dissatisfaction, and they will not tell their men that their performance was poor so as not to hurt their ego. If you do not satisfy your woman sexually, she will pretend you do and another man will do your work for you. More than 80% of women eventually cheat on their men.

Men should understand that the physiology of the woman is different from that of the man. The romantic words, glances, cuddles, quality foreplay, gifts, cruises, vacations and, dates are romantic gestures to sustain a high romantic spirit in women. Women love clothes. They are shoe-obsessed, and their eyes dilate with new clothes and pumps. Giving a woman what she wants shows the woman that you have a clue concerning style. Weave love, sex, intimacy, passion, and romance into the fabric of your daily lives. Accord your partner, the courtesy of keeping your weight in check, smelling good and looking good. These add spice to relationships and keep couples in their colorful world of romance.

5

Brain Pleasure Centers

I held him and would not let him go

The "pleasure center" is a powerful complex located in the brain. It is the general term for the set of brain structures that produce great pleasure when stimulated electrically. It comprises an array of nerves and relay interconnections that form an assembly of fascinating projections. In all humans, the "pleasure center" forms the focal point of eroticism and sensual desires, excitements, arousals, and gratification of various kinds. Pleasurable sensations affect the brain's nerve circuits that act as high speed connections to the pleasure center. The brain is also known to regulate many normal and pathological behaviors.

The "pleasure center" is a complex through which electrical signals discharge or reciprocate feelings, such as mood, amusement, longing, anticipation, anxiety, depression, fear, etc. The "pleasure center" can be stimulated by sensations of touch, smell, sight, sound, warmth, memories, and pleasurable scenarios. The brain has multiple pleasure centers and it is a wonderful thing working totally beyond human understanding.

The above exposition on this subject reveals that singles, widows, and divorced persons in protracted singlehood, could go through pangs of loneliness and depression. Unfortunately, for reasons of aging and ill health some of these persons are abandoned in rehabilitation centers, hospitals, and retirement centers. They require attention as well because the brain is constantly emitting electrical signals of moods that may need to be satisfied in their lives at such moments. An understanding of this subject and necessary interventions in the lives of these singles may improve their health and possibly prevent emotional breakdowns or severe health conditions.

Feelings and emotions are central to human behavior, and there is a biological mechanism mediating behavior motivated by events commonly associated with pleasure in humans. These events are primary factors governing normal behavior. An aspect of behavior relevant to this subject matter is the motivation relating to appetite. This concerns behavior directed toward goals that are associated with pleasure demands like sex, wine and food. Pleasure processes in the brain are known to regulate human desires and behavior.

Even desires for food trigger a special pleasure center in the brain linked with pressure to eat something you should not eat. The awareness of this is essential, especially in times of dieting as a health prescription or when there is a need to cut down on weight. The brain plays a central role in regulating human appetite for sex, wine, food and other desires. When the brain's pleasure center is activated, it sets in motion these various desires, and it requires tacit self-control to deal with these desires, which the pleasure center may be asking for.

Research has confirmed that "reward centers" in the brain prompt obese people to eat more. Singles of both sexes that have problems of obesity should, therefore, be aware of this brain function and exercise self control as much as possible in their eating habits. Singles in the dating game should be conscious of their weight and body statistics for greater appeal to their desired partners, while married couples should show courtesy to their partners by controlling their weight as well. Exercising the body and eating healthy make a sexier you.

Males for instance are more physical and visual than females. Usually, they take decisions to "prey" or "chase" the opposite sex by what they see. Obese persons of both sexes are likely to attract fewer of the opposite sex, while smart and trendy looking persons of both sexes have perhaps more appeal to the sensory organ of sight. Obese people should consult Dieticians for advice on appropriate diet. Beyond reasons of greater appeal, confidence and dating purposes, obesity may have health implications on the short or long run. Keep-fit centers should also be used because exercising the body is fundamental to good mental and physical health.

Upgrade your makeup, hair styles, and clothes from time to time with a motive to emphasize your best features and colors. Visiting barbing and beauty shops regularly is a good idea to upgrade continually ones appearance. Looking good gives a greater self-confidence and it is an ingredient to good health. Looking good is also feeling good inwardly, and it is image building as well as creating radiance around you.

Smiling represents a positive disposition toward life. Smiling has the potentials to attract friends and other smiling people, and this could alleviate feelings of loneliness. There are different kinds of smile: smiling with the eyes, closed mouth smile, smiling with cheek dimples showing, a laughing smile with teeth showing and mouth open.

Being happy and emitting smiles with either the eyes or mouth is important because someone may fall in love with your smiles. Smiles are contagious and could make someone more attractive than frowns. Smiling is a good facial exercise. It lifts the face making someone look younger, apparently sending messages from the brain to other parts of the body that "life is good."

6

The Midnight Hour

His voice knocks in the midnight hours

It was midnight, and Betty tossed and turned on her beautifully made bed in brutalized emotions. It was eerie silence. She was uncomfortable and teary eyed because she was depressed and lonely. She was trying to recuperate from a broken heart. Randy, her boyfriend of six years had said "good bye." It was lonely nights for Betty, and she dreaded the midnight hours. She was very attached to her erstwhile romantic partner, and she suffered from anxiety attacks due to their split. She had an emotional loneliness, and a lowered feeling of self-worth. Loneliness is an unpleasant feeling in which a person experiences a strong sense of emptiness and solitude resulting from inadequate levels of social relationships. Loneliness is a social pain, and it alerts someone of undesired isolation, and it motivates a longing for social connections. All that Betty wanted was Randy by her side in the midnight hours.

Betty is a quintessential society girl. She is a blonde with fair skin and light eyes. She wears sleek, sexy blond locks most of the time. Randy was the significant person in her life, and the break-up initiated a grief response in her life. Their break-up was precipitated by an unusual situation in which the feeling of love could not be reciprocated. They had a communication dysfunction, and a downward relationship spiral. She suffered romantic rejection because of Randy's preferences for Jessica whom he met when he and his friends went out on a weekend gig.

Jessica is a pop star of indefinable origin. She is a musician who played with a pop-punk music band. She was gracefully slender and a highly sexualized celeb. She is also an internationally celebrated singer, songwriter and actress. She did pretty impressive things on stage, and did songs with cheesy themes that caught Randy's fancy. She demonstrated a mastery of performance as well as a huge mass appeal. Known for her rich vocals, her vocal range is mezzo-soprano, and her record spawn the hit single spotlight. The hit track was vilified by the press. She took the pop world by quiet storm. Her rise to stardom has been meteoric and her multiple awards and unbelievable record sales are a testament to her extraordinary talent.

The songstress and pop sensation had on trendy tights and was simply intriguing. She had a fresh faced hippie look and wavy locks. She was also wearing statement earrings; the type that fashion blogs would be abuzz with. At the end of the show, as Jessica relaxed sipping a cold glass of juicy drink, Randy had an adventurous spirit and flashed Jessica a flirty smile. He made romantic overtures to her with enthusiastic candor. They got talking and her cheeks flushed as Randy asked if he could see her again. They kept company until dawn sipping a little wine and cold juicy drink. Randy escorted Jessica to her car at dawn, and kissed her goodbye with a plan to have a romantic midweek date night with her.

It was a unique blend of energy and exhilaration as they met at a posh dinner place to entertain themselves as new pals. Jessica looked fresh faced and looked truly sophisticated with her one shoulder Valentino lace dress and Brian Atwood pumps. She was wearing Piaget's "Limelight Garden Party" necklace, which is set with 204 diamonds and 128 emeralds and dreamy earrings. Randy was mesmerized by her looks and lusted after her. Love comes in three flavors: lust, romantic love, and long-term attachment. Lust involves a craving for sex. Lust is aroused more easily in men by visual stimuli than is the case for women. It is a fundamental fact that men are more attracted by youth and beauty.

Jessica looked astonishing, glitzy and gorgeous; and she provoked in Randy thrilling sensations that ran through his spine. They had a lavish dinner of French meals and wines and relaxed with traditional Irish tunes. She was exuding with cheerfulness as she told Randy of her scheduled global appearances with her music group. This was to span a period of nine months, and she was deeply involved in her rehearsals for the world tour. The pop sensation and legendry diva, best known for her music vocals would embark on her world tour in a couple of days.

Through grape vine stories, Betty knew that Randy was seeing Jessica. She knew that Randy was gone leaving her in the middle of the deep blue sea. Randy was having an utopian experience with Jessica. He stopped picking Betty's calls and sent her a card with the word "goodbye" engrained in it. It was shattered dreams for Betty who had envisioned a life with Randy. It was excruciating pain as Betty had flashbacks of a onetime romantic relationship. Her ears could hear Randy's deep voice "knocking" in the midnight hours as she drifted into romantic fantasies of the past. She remembered Randy's love and how they both lie cuddled by the fireplace at winter seasons sipping Bolinger and staring lovingly into each other's eyes. It was anguish for Betty whose heart palpitated wildly as the brutal arrows of rejection pierced her fragile heart.

Betty sobbed profusely as she re-lived the feelings of a romantic rejection, and she occasionally glanced at the clock hanging on the cold walls of her bedroom. It was midnight, and a rainy night with tears raining from her eyes. The rain drops caused her some chills. As the tears rolled down her pallid cheeks, giddy feelings overwhelmed her as she sobbed profusely. She needed some warmth, and she made her way to the fireplace. Sleep eluded her as she had grueling nostalgic feelings of Randy. As she paced the room, she clung onto Randy's kerchief, which was in her purse the night that Randy bade her goodbye.

The aroma of his own unique fragrance sparked immediate nostalgia, and she became teary-eyed. Randy was her hero, her heartthrob, and electrifying radiance.

Days went by, and she detested the midnight hours because excruciating pains of separation from her beloved troubled her sleep. She ate sparingly and dreaded the midnight hours. The doctors diagnosed her with insomnia and anorexia. She was put on tranquilizing pills to soothe her frayed nerves and aching heart. She developed midnight anxiety attacks and hibernated within the cold walls of her home. She agonized the mishap, and would cling unto her pillows listening to the beats of her palpitating heart.

At twilight, she would look through her windows for hours unending remembering the times when Randy pulled up at her drive way for his romantic visits. Who would take the place of Randy; she wondered in the midnight hours. She would toss and turn on her lonely bed, teary-eyed till dawn. She became an emotional wreck who had to fight back tears whenever she spoke about her troubled love life. She took time off work to nurse her wounded heart. Dejection and gloom enveloped her, and she began to develop withdrawal tendencies. Uncontrollably, she drifted into depression and solitude. She sought for solitude up in the mountains; so as to get away from human habitation. Living became a harrowing experience.

Jessica, Randy's new heartthrob was to make the first appearance for her music world tour at the Hotel Arcade in London where a mammoth crowd was expected. Randy flew into London on a cool summer evening to watch the song diva perform for the London audience. She is an artist who inspires her global fan base every day. The event was a huge success and Randy was her guest at her hotel suite where she relaxed at midnight after the intriguing show.

It was a euphoric midnight experience as Randy and Jessica were lost in ecstatic bedroom adventures. They took time to inhale the sensual aroma of the dimly lit hotel bedroom, which light effects sedated their nerves, and endorphins were released. The singing sensation sang bluesy tunes into Randy's ears that tingled his body. They made love all night long, and had a sumptuous breakfast on bed at the hotel suite at mid-morning. Randy bade her goodbye at dusk to catch a flight for North America where he had crucial executive meetings with his business partners.

Jessica had another scheduled appearance in Wales a fortnight later, and Randy flew on a first class ticket to

Wales to support his new found love. It was a gruesome flight as the captain of the aircraft announced that there was thunderstorm and that there could be emergency landing. There was pandemonium in the air as the pilot struggled to make a safe landing with his five crew members and 84 passengers on board. It was scary and harrowing as the plane made a tumultuous but safe landing.

Keeping up with his promise to be with Jessica for yet another music show, Randy rode an airport cab to be with his new found love before her music performance. He heaved a sigh of relief for a safe landing as he made his way to Jessica's hotel suite. On his way, however, he had a strange feeling of exhaustion and sudden flashbacks of Betty. Randy remembered Betty, his lost love. He remembered the sweet and peaceful moments he had shared with Betty. He broke his several week-long silence as he text-messaged her to ask how she was doing and if she was seeing someone else. He informed Betty that he was in England but would arrive in North America at midweek. He offered candid apologies to Betty for their break-up. He indicated having dinner with her at the weekend when he returns.

Betty was bewildered and euphoric when she received the text message. The text came in at midnight and Betty got into sexual fantasies of Randy all over again. Nostalgic feelings of their romantic lives consumed her as she had flash-backs of his deep voice whispering "Betty I am all yours." She remembered the thrilling moments with Randy, and the thought of seeing Randy again was all entrancing. Randy was her first love, and being enveloped in his arms was all that mattered to Betty. It was great expectations as Betty waited for that moment with Randy. Before the relationship hit the skids, it was sizzling romance for the two love birds. They had a combination of passionate and compassionate love, and a demonstration of strong affection. When you fall in love, it is a temporary madness. It erupts like an earthquake and it subsides. Love itself is what is left over, when being in love has burned away.

It was romance again as Randy hooked up with Betty. Randy picked up from the florist a bouquet of red dahlias flowers, which he presented to Betty on their re-union date. Betty had a forgiving heart because loving ignites a range of human emotions. Loving is like being caught up in the spider's web helpless, and you become a slave to the object of your love. Romance is about aiming cupid's arrow straight at the heart of your partner and watching your heart's "best dish" fall in love with you over and over again. Romance is as inexplicable as the beauty of a rainbow.

Betty's heart was racing as she caught sight of Randy. The internal elixir of love is responsible for making our hearts race when we come in contact with the one that is holding us captive. Randy was profuse over Betty because she was more of his ideal woman. He could not cope with Jessica's cumbersome world music tours and frivolous living. He had missed Betty's soothing and balmy love. It was genuine love, and Randy craved for a long-term attachment to Betty as love flows from the deep springs of the heart. Betty is very effeminate, loving, and caring with a pleasant disposition. She responds positively to Randy's success at work and business. Their sweet re-union was enigmatic, and reflected a sense of togetherness.

Randy and Betty agreed to meet at the VIP lounge of the Hilton Hotels on a beautiful summer afternoon. Betty arrived surprisingly simple with smoky eyes, full brow, pink blush, and glossy pink lips. It was another whirlwind romance as they spend quality time at the VIP lounge. They took a walk into the beautiful gardens and waterfalls at the Hilton where they beheld the azure of the skies once again. Walking through the gardens, it was passionate glances at each other as they hand-in-hand took relaxed steps to the lounge. It was another adorable moment for the reconciled pair as love for each other flowed from the deep springs of their hearts.

Randy, smiling out of genuine delight proposed to Betty; pledging to be the man of her dreams. When Randy proposed, they went to a park that has a beautiful view of the city and took a familiar trail to a resting place and had lunch. It was a Lorraine Schwartz engagement ring of her dreams. Betty was overwhelmed with love as she shared the best moments of her life with Randy. They were at the beach at the weekend, and they had a mind-blowing time together. They agreed to have a beach wedding during the summer season. Beaches are the paradise of lovers and couples. Lovers should be inventive, and explore numerous ways of finding pleasure. There are many events that lovers can plan together that will keep their love lives inflamed and ecstatic.

Betty was floating in the galaxies with imaginations of her dream wedding becoming a reality. They chose a unique small wedding venue offering the best beach weddings in Florida. A marriage on a beach is exciting and stimulating. They want to be in a relaxed, casual mood, and feel the pleasure of sandy seashore. They got the beach wedding experts to put the wedding together. They had a sunset wedding ceremony and a good set up for the sweetest memories. Their wedding was the greatest fete of the season. The couple's pink and white cake was a six-foot tall, pink and white masterpiece.

Betty looked every inch a blushing bride in a body hugging white strapless dress. She had long stemmed flowers tied with a satin ribbon for that fashionable look. She was simple yet trendy, and was dressed up in white with some pearls and sequins. They gave their vows a personal touch, and shared their wedding day in front of cameras. It was an elegant and memorable beach wedding and reception. Their guests enjoyed themselves and stayed cool in the warm and humid weather of the beachside. It was pleasure again at midnight as Randy and Betty gave themselves the best of each other in their romantic bedroom that had cool lights and soft music. It was midnight euphoria for Betty as she clung desperately to Randy's body mesmerized by the midnight thrills.

7

One-Shoulder Hug

I will not forget the thrills of yesterday

Hugging is a perfect interaction between people which brings bodies into close contact with one another. In coming close together, you effectively "become one" joining identities for a few moments. A perfect hug is a close, genuine, and intimate act. A hug is to clasp tightly in the arms, especially with affection. It is clinging firmly to something that is cherished. It is a close affectionate embrace and an outward expression of love. Hugging is a touch of love and can feel great and greatly improve lover's mood. It is a warm embrace and can ignite the activities of the love hormones oxytocin and vasopressin in lovers. Hugging is an intimate form of touch, which is a compliment to your partner.

Women love smoothness and chivalry. A hug flows out naturally with an easy giving and receiving. A touch by the object of our affection or a wrap of our lover's arms around us could cause a gush of oxytocin. Oxytocin is a potent "bonding" hormone secreted by the pituitary glands. Lovers have a profound physical and emotional need for touch. By hugging someone, you remind them that you care about them and support them. Hugging gives lovers the feeling that the two of them are the only people who matter at that moment. Hugging is one of the best gifts your guy can give to you because he transmits his warmth to you for a brief moment. A hug can be just as intimate as a kiss, and it is an important expression of affection.

When your guy gives you a romantic hug, your arms should be around his neck and shoulders, and he should be embracing you around the waist and lower back. He can lift you up in a crush hug while pressing you gently against his body. Squeezing and lifting you are expressions of delight. Your guy can give you a long, loving hug, and you should go along until he lets you go. You should maintain the hugged position for a brief moment and let go with a smile. If the situation is fitting, he should look you in the eyes and kiss you as he means it, including a gentle hair massage. He can go a step further by giving you a small massage with his hands. This will make you feel better about yourself and surroundings.

On the other hand, a one-shoulder hug from your guy is a sign that he is "distancing" himself from you in the relationship. It is a good indicator that he is telling you a whopper. It is also an indicator that his passion and love for you is dwindling. A one-shoulder hug is a hug that a guy did not just care to give. It is a sign that he is retreating from you. Soft eye contacts are not made during a one-shoulder hug and hugging is a key part of any romantic relationship. Hugging is a non-verbal form of communication; it is valuable, and it increases intimacy. If it is done without passion, he is indicating that you are just buds and should not take the relationship with him seriously. A hug is to give someone a sign of love but a one-shoulder hug is to hug someone with an arm over one shoulder. It is worthy to note that a friend hug is different from a lover hug.

Natalie fell in love with Nick on Christmas Eve when they met at a Happy Hour event to usher in the Christmas day. Natalie was in the company of her girlfriends as they sat on the high sits of the bar doing wine tasting. It was like a girls' night for Natalie and her friends who were coxing some fun for the festive period. Natalie is a passionate and vivacious artist with a voracious appetite for life and love. A sleek city girl, Natalie stood out among her friends because she was wearing a dress with bold colors that emphasized her incredible figure.

She was wearing a sky blue gown embellished by a flowing ribbon of purple, looking clean, crisp, and rich. The absolutely divine and extravagant blue dress made her look smashing. It was an iconic dress of all time. Her hair was supplemented by weaving in sleek, natural-looking faux-hair pieces to get beautiful looking effects. She has appeared on countless magazine covers for developing a great body and good burst line. She has a distinctive sex appeal and was most luscious among her friends.

Nick was sitting alone on a table for two, sipping some brandy. It was the Christmas season, and the weather was cold and icy. At the strike of the minute before midnight, people took to the dance floor in euphoric excitement of the dawn of the Christmas day. Natalie made some "peacocking moves" on the dance floor. She was dancing alone expressing herself through her body and that caught the fancy of Nick as men are more easily aroused by visual stimuli. Nick came close by to join her on the dance floor, and they smiled with their eyes. He conveyed his love with a radiant style and a direct soft eye contact.

They were on the dance floor as the midnight rolled into a new day. He wooed her romantically and got a consenting response from Natalie. Nick bade Natalie goodbye with a warm hug at dawn. The warmth of his body was a good feeling and that made lasting impressions in Natalie's mind. When two people are attracted to each other and by each other, a virtual frenzy of hormone and neurochemical activity occurs. Their brief romance at the dancing floor helped them to recapture the essence of what it is like to be in love.

Nick began to see Natalie, and they appeared a promising pair. They scheduled a vacation to the Canary Islands at summer time because Nick needed to relax from his highly demanding job. He is a film and television actor as well as a reality star that appears on various reality television series. In their lovely hotel room far away in the Canary Islands, they had moments when they glided into ecstasy. It became a colorful world, and Nick was enthusiastic about her. As they beheld the silky skies in the Islands, they would hear the sound of the chirping birds. They developed a profoundly tender and passionate affection for each other.

It was an exhilarating experience as they cruised on the boats and enjoyed some aquatic life. On one of their sea adventures, they met some guys on a boat looking at them through binoculars, and this made them keep indoors in their posh hotel swimming pool. Wearing a Maillot swim suit, Natalie had the best as she swam for physical fitness and to calm her nerves. She is a fitness guru who had introduced Nick to visiting the fitness centers for the thread mill walk. Nick treated Natalie with much ardor, and it was a luscious vacation and a romantic get-a-way.

When they arrived from the Canary Islands, Nick went back to his busy job schedule and dated Natalie at the weekends. At midweeks, they would meet in a local bookstore for coffee, and she will enjoy profuse warm hugs from Nick at each meeting. Nick would clasp her in his arms for a brief moment and whisper his appreciation each time they met there. It was a spicy and intriguing relationship. She loves him up every chance she gets. The theater was his great love and Natalie identified with his passion. During their ultimate weekend hideout, they watched sensuous adult movies with glee because it rekindled their romantic spirit. They also relaxed at the unique bungalow, which combined the privacy and comfort of a luxury home with exceptional services and unparalleled amenities. Reciprocating her gestures of love, Nick gave Natalie a surprise birthday bash at the beach near his Malibu home.

Natalie was hopeful of a lifelong relationship with Nick as he introduced her to his family and friends. Natalie featured in Nick's family life and joined them on holiday cruises and beach outings. Natalie was looking forward to a marriage proposal from Nick, which will be her most romantic moment with Nick. Nick has a matured disposition and led a somewhat sedentary social life because of a busy work schedule. Nick as an introvert had blended well with Natalie's extrovert qualities. Natalie had her dream wedding in mind and went window shopping for wedding dresses and rings occasionally. She would gaze through the show glasses for wedding rings in the famous wedding shops in town. She would act out those fantasies of a great engagement and life with Nick.

Nick had spoilt Natalie with romantic hugs and gestures. He was a man of few words but demonstrated his love with outward expressions of love. Spontaneous kissing, hand holding, and hugs were features of their romantic lives. They had sizzling moments at the weekend to relax from the week's stress. Their relationship was the most exciting of Natalie's romantic adventures and Nick was her heart's best friend and hero. Her cheeks would flush, her heart would race, and her palms would sweat at the sight of Nick. Nick was clearly her heartthrob whom she hoped to be with for the rest of her life. Extreme excitement engulfed her each time she got herself ready for their romantic evenings.

It was the beginning of autumn, and Nick organized a canapé style reception for his brother's birthday. Their friends and family were at the venue to grace the occasion. Natalie made frantic event preparations. She had to drive a long way to get Nick his favorite ice cream flavor for the occasion; because she expresses her love ever so often to Nick. She looked radiant and smashing in a pink flowing gown and dreamy eye shadows.

On arrival at the birthday celebrations, she approached her sweetheart with wide open arms for the usual romantic and assuring hug but Nick gave her a one-shoulder hug and her blood congealed within her body. Surprised at the frosty reception and seeming romantic rejection, she withdrew into her cocoon during the occasion flabbergasted at what might have gone wrong. Their frosty greeting puzzled the audience. As she braced up to hop into her car at the end of the party, she received another casual hug from Nick as he thanked her for gracing the occasion. As Natalie drove home in her Lexus Sports, she was teary-eyed and bewildered; wondering where things went wrong.

Nick's one-shoulder hug bothered Natalie as Nick kept his distance and maintained an eerie silence. It was a difficult time for Natalie as she tried to hold back tears at the romantic rejection she went through with Nick. Her fingers would cringe, and she would convulse in feverish chills as she remembered their ecstatic date nights. It was difficult to fall in love again for Natalie. Her social life became uneventful as she concentrated her energies in the world of work. Her income improved, and she was able to afford brief vacations for a change of environment.

Vacations have beneficial psychological and therapeutic effects with potentials to reduce stress triggered health ailments. The vacations reduced the toll of stress and loneliness on Natalie because it took her away from the work mindset. Consequently, her work performance improved after each vacation because she spent time relaxing in her get-a-away. This helped her forget the emotional traumas of the past, and she became ready to have a social life again. Connecting with her friends to attend the gigs again, she met Nick on one of these occasions. She made eye contact with Nick and that triggered their old feelings for each other. Nick came over and clasped her tightly in his arms, and she became breathless. It was an intimate and warm hug that was delightful. It was a touch of love, and an affectionate embrace. Nick would not let her go, and in breathy whispers promised to love her all over again.

8

A Romantic Bed Room

A romantic bed is a happy bed to visit each night.

A romantic room will spice up your relationship, and a romantic bed is a happy bed to visit each night. Lovers and newly weds deserve a bedroom fit for royalty with an ultra-romantic look. Your bedroom should represent your unique style, and couples should be design savvy. Your bedroom must inspire romance and intimacy because romance is the garden on which lovers sit. It is the real deal that keeps a relationship juicy. Your bedroom should be a seductive space capable of arousing the five senses of touch, sight, taste, smell and hearing.

Make your bedroom peaceful and beautiful with luscious and creative furniture. Your bedroom should be a dream home where you will always want to come back to. Redecorate and make changes to your bedroom always because it is where the magic happens. Erect a life-size picture of yourself in the sexiest outfit in your bedroom. Have music at the background always in your bedroom because music is a vital part of a romantic moment. Listen to romantic audio tapes with your partner for its potentials to arouse. Your bedroom should have a bit of color because it is where you and your spouse retreat for rest, relaxation and romance. Create a haven of a bedroom with harmonious color combinations.

Make the bed your showpiece and have a few "throw pillows" to give your bed some personality. Extra throw pillows give plushness to the bed, and they give a soothing and alluring feel to the body. Your bed should look inviting, attractive and flattering, and lighting can make your room sexier. A clean well-made bed with crystal lights is very tempting and fascinating. Your beddings should look alluring like a fluffy cloud. Treat your body right with soft sheets for a softer and smoother feel. This will give sweet comfort to the love birds during their romantic moments.

Create romantic vibes in your bedroom by installing dimmers and colored shades over bed lamps. Candles also change the lighting and set the scene of love. Fragrance scented candles and crystal chandelier hanging in front of the bed gives a romantic look to the bedroom. Add some glamour by hanging an extra dimmable chandelier. Soft light is much more flattering than bright over head lights at bed time. Soft and cool lights set the right romantic environment for lovers, and love making becomes a desirable and fascinating experience. Flicker flame bulbs in the bedroom give an alluring feel as well. Have good drapes or blinds for privacy, and to keep out the sunlight whenever the two of you want to spend the day in bed. Silk or velvet drapes are soft looking and romantic. Drapes or shades will help shut the world out so that you can concentrate on your romance; because romance is the real deal that keeps the relationship juicy.

Create that romantic ambiance by placing bouquets of fresh flowers on the nightstands. You can scatter rose petals on the bed and bedroom floor to celebrate your birthdays or wedding anniversaries. Hang photos that remind you both of your love story and the wonderful memories you have shared. Turn your bedroom into a "boudoir" by using soft colors and fabrics, and stick fresh flowers on the mirrors. Floor length mirrors in the bedroom create wonderful reflective surface that adds beauty and depth. Make your bed the star of the room, and the focal point. It should stand out and be warm and welcoming for you and your spouse. Turn your room to your favorite vacation destination and re-kindle vacation memories.

Keep your bedroom doors closed always to shut out noise and other distractions, and try having late-night champagne and snacks in bed for that soothing delight. Your bedroom should convey warmth, comfort, luxury, and intimacy because that is where you begin and end the day. Your bedroom should be perfect and tantalizing for both relaxation and romance because that is where the magic happens.

9

I'm Your Lady!

And You're Mine

L ove truly is a mystery. It is a mystery why we fall in love. A mystery how it happens, and a greater mystery how it comes. It is a mystery why love grows, and a mystery why it fails. Love impresses the mind with a sense of inspiring awe about the object of love. Loving is intoxication and is capable of generating feelings that can penetrate the silky clouds. Love blooms and blossoms when it is appreciated and reciprocated. When it is reciprocated, love is mystical, and could get to ecstatic dimensions with the couple transcending into convulsive feelings for each other. The person we are lovingly drawn to is a living mystery at that moment in time. At least once in your life time, the gift of love will come to you in full flowers. This ecstatic feeling could disarm someone of all logical reasoning.

Love is moving from a feeling of neutrality toward someone to one of love. The word "fall" that is often associated with love means an uncontrollable feeling towards someone. Love is to be delighted about the happiness of another person. The components of love are both feelings and activity toward someone you love. Love is a profound longing for someone, and it is mostly tender and quiet. Loving is delightful, fulfilling, and a tremendous passion for someone. It is hopelessness and helplessness, and a feeling that consumes your being.

Loving is mystifying and stupefying typified by eccentric imaginations of the object of your love. It is a beautiful romantic feeling, which sends electrifying sensations through the nerves of the human body. Loving is a strange and explosive feeling that assumes irrational crescendos, and could leave the person in love basking in the sun hopelessly like the "lotus eaters." Loving is capable of keeping the lover awake through the midnight hours in amazing wonder of the object of love; totally blinded of reality. This is because feelings and emotions are central to human behavior. However, when the scales fall off the eyes, the dawn of reality welcomes the song "I can see clearly now that the rain is gone."

Love is a human issue and a social phenomenon. Love is influenced by certain body hormones. At the height of romantic affections, the body responds by secreting some chemicals. Sexual attraction and a longing for attachment is a strong drive for love. Deep and true love is a combination of both compassionate love and passionate love. Compassionate love is intense affection for someone with a strong desire to give love and care for the object of our love. True love most of the time takes time to build up. Curiosity, patience, acceptance, and seeing people for who they truly are remain important components of compassionate love.

Passionate love is an intense longing for intimacy with someone. Arousal feelings like shortness of breath, rapid heart rate accompany passionate love. Passionate love alone does not sustain relationships for a long time. This is because it burns off too quickly, especially when the instant desires have been fulfilled. However, a combination of compassionate and passionate love is required for more wholesome and enduring relationships, which is a solid foundation for long lasting marriages.

Love is an intense interpersonal attraction. Love is a deep feeling of tenderly care for another person. Love is a very passionate desire for someone that could entail either desire for romantic love or to a non-sexual emotional closeness, which is platonic love. Love is a direct contrast with lust and infatuation. You become breathless and develop some erotic feelings toward someone you love. Love is a "light" that allows people to see things that are not seen by others, and love makes you disproportionately magnify the qualities of the one you love.

Love matters are difficult to comprehend, and the exact origin of the desire to love is not known. Love matters are capable of provoking various abnormalities to your behavior. When you are intensely in love, you compromise rather too quickly because you do not want to lose or hurt the target of your love. When you are intensely in love, your emotions may become uncontrollable, and at this point you have lost the sense of sound reasoning and judgment. You become more gullible and stand the risk of being easily manipulated.

Love comes with a sense of responsibility if you desire to keep the person you love for the rest of your life. Issues of love are capable of making you anxious, and you could break down emotionally and get into health conditions. This is because love plays the most important role in your life. When you are in love, you are like a blind slave of the person who has imprisoned your heart. Love is real, and it dates back to the origin of man.

Love comes with possibly agreeing to do the most absurd things to possess the person you desire, to keep them near you even if they do not want to, to block their freedom, to make them love you in return. Sometimes, you want to force various situations to your favor and many things more, only because you desperately need to be near this person and keep him or her near you as long as you live. You also have a burning desire to express yourself and unfold your sensibilities to the person you love. Susceptibility to sensory stimuli becomes obvious and sometimes overwhelming.

Loving could make you hallucinate, giggle, and smile at the mere thoughts of the one you love. When you are in love, erstwhile dormant hormones could begin to rage. Chemical reactions in the body and the raging hormones could catapult you to a horizon where you are captivated with only the thoughts of the one you love. You do not pay attention to any details anymore, and you no longer can think logically because you prefer to be involved in the magical feeling that your emotions present. You are constantly drifting into utopia (your own fantasy world) as you caress the issues surrounding your love in your heart. You become so vulnerable at this point that you cannot accept to stay far from the person you desire so much.

The inexplicable nature of love and its unknown origin makes it a mystery. Love as a social phenomenon is both natural and universal. Love is potent, and potentially powerful to pilot thoughts about the object of your love. Love holds you bound and entranced about the object of your love. It keeps you thrilled and transfixed at the mere thought of the one you love. Loving is a good feeling, especially when it is reciprocated. Reciprocated love gives good health and sweet long life. Giving your lady sweet loving, will keep her constantly coming back for more of you!

10

Springy Wedding
In Paris

~ Sweet matrimony ~

Marriage is a beautiful garden
A garden of beautiful flowers
Flowers with enticing flavors
Flavors that partners smell with delight
Delight of a life time
A life time of caring
A life time of cuddling

A life time of romance
A life time of giving
A life time of bliss
A life time of sweet whispers
A lifetime of desire
Desire for my beloved
My beloved who is mine
My beloved that I can trust
My beloved that I can lean on
In times that I am weary
In times I have a need
A need for love!

There is something romantic about the spring season. Coming out of the deepest darkest winter, and embracing light and color makes us feel delightfully different in spring. Springtime is a wonderful time in the year with the advent of warmer weather. Spring signifies the emergence of a new life. There are newly budding leaves and spots of green sprouting from the ground. Spring months are the blossoming months that bring meaningful growth and rejuvenation in its wake. Spring is a time to wake up, and spring back into action and sprightliness. It is the time to let the sunshine into your life again. With the warm weather, you can pack a picnic, and clutch onto your partner's arms again screaming playfully through the part and reconnect on an exciting level.

Dusting yourself from the winter blues, spring raises the hopes of romance again. It is a time of spotting a humming bird, and watching bees land on flowers. It is a time to bring out those colorful sundresses and pumps, and treat yourself to a warm weather mani-and-pedi. As you update your spring wardrobe, your partner gets fascinated at you again. It is a time to wear those eye-popping color bra and panty, and rub on some scented lotion. Your lover will like seeing your skin on display for the first time in months, and it will help to regenerate that sexual energy that has been on hiatus during the lurid winter months.

Wedding is a dream come true for Carol and Jerry, and they wanted to spring-clean their romance and breathe new life into their sexual connection. They had intriguing dreams about their lives together, and wanted to have a spring romance in Paris. Spring time is a time of sails on the river and drives or walks through the parks in and around the city of Paris. Paris, one of the world's major global cities is one of the most livable and expensive cities in Europe. Paris is the most visited city in the world, and it has many tourist attractions. There are also country clubs that dot the suburbs of the city and these features hold great attraction for Jerry and Carol.

They planned a honeymoon and spring wedding for an exhilarating breath of springtime romance in Paris. Their wedding was to celebrate their unique love story, and to have an over-the-top romantic wedding. Jerry and Carol have lived in the Netherlands all their lives. It was love at first sight when they met in the Winepress. Jerry gave Carol a sexy smile, and they fell head over heels in love with each other. Jerry was 27 and Carol was 25. Jerry is one of the highest paid professional athletes in Netherlands. He inherited an expansive housing estate from his family, and he is a great person. He is a man of the net while Carol is a buxom reality star.

Within six months of whirlwind romance, Jerry proposed to Carol. Under crystal lights in Jerry's multimillion dollar home, Jerry whispered into her ears a soft request to marry him. Carol stared at him with piercing dreamy eyes; overwhelmed with rapturous delight. It was great expectations as they made arrangements for the most eventful day of their lives.

They invited celebrity guests who were delightfully steeped with warmth and charm. It was over-the-top celebrity wedding, and an all-star event that was contracted to wedding planners. They arranged private jets to fly the wedding guests to Paris from the Netherlands, and all the wedding guests were to lodge in exquisite hotels. It was all glamour as the creative wedding planners used a team of floral designers to design the wedding hall with flower patches on the floor. They transformed the wedding venue into a visually stimulating wonderland.

Jerry wore a white, peak lapel tuxedo jacket with black tuxedo pants while Carol wore a mermaid Kleinfeld wedding dress. The wedding ring was a Tiffany wedding band embellished with gem stones. The strapless gown complemented her complexion perfectly. She wore an elbow length veil with lace and crystal accents. Her facial makeup was igniting, and luscious. Her maid of honor wore a definitive designer dress by Jovani. Their cake was a fabulous seven-foot tall burgundy and cream masterpiece.

Carol arrived at the wedding venue with sparkling eyes, a glowing skin, and sizzling smiles. Their wedding was the greatest fete in Paris during the spring season. It was an all-star event with great highlights. When Jerry kissed his bride, doves were released into the air and that created an exciting moment for the wedding guests. They screamed with rapturous delight as the doves ascended to the skies. The doves appeared as a cluster of white feathers up the skies and the guests re-positioned themselves for the most exciting view of the romantic scene. They enjoyed the champagne toast in a special outdoor niche and invited the guests outdoors to watch the sunset. After the wedding, Carol ventured outside to throw her bouquet of flowers into the crowd, and dance in front of a of forest of TV cameras.

Sitting on the outdoor lounge, they were filled with ecstatic delight at the most romantic event of their lives. While on the lounge, there was an explosive surprise from their friends when fireworks filled the evening sky. These moments infused their celebration with romance, making it a splashy wedding. It was a charming and cheesy wedding, and a major glitz and glam in Paris. It was also a celebration of the magic and wonder of spring in Paris. They posed for their photos on their sleek modern lounge. After Carol and her fabulous beau's nuptials, they proceeded to a swanky hotel for their two-week springtime honeymoon. After their glitzy wedding and super-luxe honeymoon in Paris, Carol, and Jerry scheduled to be back to the garden suites in Paris for their first wedding anniversary. It was a post wedding bliss with intense pleasurable moments. They treated themselves to great luxury and delighted themselves with the finest of French wines and delicacies. As they flew back to the Netherlands, the passions of the springy wedding in Paris remained indelible in their minds.

11

If You Treat Me Right

I will be all yours

Every woman has embedded innately in her heart a desire to be treated right. When you treat a woman right, she will be all yours. Men and women have different emotional wiring. Men and women have different stressors and the brain seems to have evolved to be in tune with those different stressors. While men and women have basically the same hardware, it is the software instructions and how they are put to use that make the sexes seem different. Where the anatomy of the brain is concerned, men and women do think differently.

The brain is made primarily of two different types of tissue called gray matter and white matter. Men think more with their gray matter and the women the white. Men and women have different experiences with pain. Women report more pain throughout their lives. Compared to men, women feel pain in more areas of their body and for longer durations. Men have higher pain thresholds and higher pain tolerances. This is due to the genetic and biochemical differences between men and women.

Women have peculiar emotional disposition totally different from that of men. The seat of a woman's soul is her emotions while the seat of a man's' soul is his purpose. Women enjoy reciprocity in feelings, and not just receptacles for a man's "release." Women often require a feeling of closeness and care before they can give the best of themselves. This is not necessarily care directly related to sex or the number of rounds of sexual "bouts" a man can give a woman; but rather doing things for her and making life easier for her. Women need their husband's time, attention, and affectionate touch. All these rekindle the sensual spirit of a relationship, and emphasize what it is like to be in love.

Women also have personal problems that can interfere with love relationships, and this is no fault of theirs. This can also manifest beyond relationship issues and spill into work or school problems. Drugs, alcohol or other health conditions is not the cause but rather it is a function of their biological make up, and this makes them distinctly different from men. Men should be aware of this fact and go the extra mile to pep up the woman's best feelings at all times. All women have ovaries. As soon as a woman is capable of sexual reproduction of children, (which is as from age 12 in most females), the ovaries start releasing estrogen, and this coordinates the menstruation cycle. Estrogen acts everywhere in a woman's body, including the parts of the brain that control emotions. Estrogen's actions are too complex in the woman's body, and it also modifies both the production and effects of the "feel good" chemicals in the brain. Estrogen levels fluctuate in the body and this is closely linked with women's emotional well-being.

This can manifest in mood disruptions like depression and anxiety, and this condition occur only in women. Women could experience the most unpleasant symptoms before their periods, and this is known as the premenstrual syndrome. After the menstrual period of a woman, these physical and emotional symptoms go away.

The obvious physical symptoms are breast tenderness, bloating or swelling of the arms or legs. Emotional disturbances could be anger, irritability and anxiety. Women sometimes withdraw from social activities at this time due to emotional upheavals. Women who have attained menopause have improved moods because at this time in their lives, estrogen levels are very low.

Women think differently from the way men think, and they have different biological make ups. In relationships and love situations, women could have different responses. Women are more tender and passionate than men in these circumstances and things that do not excite men may excite them. This understanding will help men who are in love and who wish to love to have more successes in relationships. Women have a tendency to dwell in the world of utopia, a world of fantasy, and they could imagine things that do not really exist when they are in love. Women normally are very romantic creatures, and they love things that are thrilling and colorful like flowers, perfumes, gifts, soft music, dating events, vacations, weddings, engagements, honeymoons, etc. Women have expectations that are uniquely women's during celebrations of valentine days, birth days, festivals, etc.

Domestic responsibilities that women are faced with daily sometimes become hectic and monotonous. Home keeping, pregnancies and child rearing are overwhelming responsibilities of women. Unknowingly these remove the spices in a once romantic relationship. In relationships, men should understand this aspect that interferes with women's emotions, and try as much as they can within the limits of their income to satisfy these aspects of women's expectations. Taking a woman on a date or relaxation trip would break a life of routine, and romantic rhythms would be restored.

Women are sweetly disposed to romance, tender caresses, treats, surprises, and outward demonstrations of love in public or in private, and all these prepare women for satisfactory sexual performance. Women are more elated and happier in these circumstances, and they tend to give the best of themselves when these things are in place. These are ingredients for longevity of marital unions and relationships in general.

As from puberty age (18 years), girls begin to cry more than boys. By age 18, women cry four times as much as men. This is caused by the presence of the hormone called prolactin which is more prevalent in women, and it contributes to how much people cry. Crying is an emotional reaction, a normal response, and it is uniquely a human phenomenon. Crying can be triggered by grief, joy, fear, remorse, frustration, humor, laughter, etc. Women, however, are known to cry more than men and in most cultures it is socially acceptable for women to cry much more than men. Strong emotions like sorrow or extreme happiness (elation) may lead to crying. When women are under strong emotional stress, suffering, or personal pain they are more likely to cry. In some instances, they may shed the "crocodile's tears." In other for some women to attract attention, they may cry and release sobbing sounds, and this most of the time attract male curiosity, passion and tenderness toward women.

Women are known to reproduce and nurture mankind. Their social activities most of the time revolve around family members. In going through situations that are peculiarly women's, the fact that they cry should not be seen as weakness. It should be understood that their physiological make up make them more prone than males in this human behavior. Two-thirds of people diagnosed with depression all over the world are women, and crying brings relief to them. Crying is, therefore, beneficial to women's health. On the other hand, women who do not wish to cry should think of something that makes them laugh or they could try long, slow, deep breathing.

When a man falls in love with a woman, he gives her easy access to his self-esteem. Men take words more literally than women and hear them in sweeping terms. Criticism can demolish a man's self-esteem. A man will try to live up to the image that his wife has of him. A woman has more influence over her man than she thinks. Men speak the language of hopes and dreams because the seat of a man's soul is his intent or purpose. A woman often marries a man for his potential. A man's ego is very vulnerable. The male ego's impact on his sexual behavior is a fuse. What a woman does can either lite the fuse, or put it out entirely. When a man's partner does not enhance his ego, he looks for where his ego is enhanced. Men need to know that they are desired.

In treating women right, it is necessary to understand that some women submit to the sexual advances of their men out of duty, and not as mutual desire. When women get to this point, sex has become uneventful, and perhaps painful because the woman's vagina would not be sufficiently lubricated for mutual pleasurable intercourse. The supposedly sweet act becomes a harrowing experience for the woman who has to painfully bear the man's thrusts until he gratifies his sexual appetite. This is raping the woman, as it were because it is innately against her will at that time.

Sex means two different things to men and women. A male needs sexual release upper and foremost. This is just plain raw sex, and he doesn't care where it comes from. His body is pouring chemicals to his brain to cause a driving need for sexual release, which makes sex an emergency for men. This need is as real as his requirement for food, and his appetite. Men must accept that women look at sex entirely differently than they do, and must meet the woman's needs before they can expect a mutual appetite for sex. Women are very exciting but the conditions have to be exactly right for sex to occur. A man should meet the woman's expectation of long-time care to be able to get mutual appetite for sex, and if a woman treats a man right, enhancing his ego, he will keep coming home.

12

Reviving
The Romance

Love is a spider waiting to entangle its victim

Romantic love is the highest form of love between two soul mates who are also lovers. It involves in its full expression, the reciprocal response of the total being of one individual to the total being of another individual. No matter how good your relationship with your partner is, there is always room for a little bit more romance. Life has a way of chipping away at our marriages:

jobs and job related travels, in-laws, activities with the children, domestic chores, financial issues, conflict and misunderstandings. Couples actually should endeavor to reconcile the erotic with the domestic, thereby, putting the chemistry back into their relationship. The truth is that couples begin to take themselves and their bodies for granted without realizing that a wear and tear is taking place in their marriages. To have a great relationship is some good work; work that is a joy when everything comes together.

Couples should realize the need to nourish and revive the love bonds that united them as lovers in the very beginning. Nourishing the relationship is a doing performance that requires effective participation of both partners. For most people, romantic relationships are the most meaningful element in their lives. Partners must work together to make the union a happy and enduring one, and they should not have a competitive urge. The best marriages are based on deep friendships. Couples should avoid conflicting schedules; so that they will have ample time to connect romantically. Alone-time unites and refreshes couples because they can relax without interruptions for a while.

In this age and time, modern life puts undue pressure on marital life. Breaking the yoke of boredom in a stale marriage requires that the couples reconnect each week doing the things they did during courtship. Just sleeping together at night time is not enough romantic activity for couples. It could become a boring routine. Couples should have romantic midweek date nights or weekend romantic gate-away to spice their relationship. Small and seemingly insignificant gestures can help keep a relationship on track. A little gift, an off-hand compliment, non-verbal communication and a moment of physical contact can vastly strengthen a relationship.

These little displays of interest and affection are fundamental in sustaining a love relationship. Verbalizing your feelings to your partner in the course of the day prepares a couple for ecstatic moments. It makes your partner feel secure, cared for, and wanted in the relationship. Physical intimacy acts of placing your hand on the thigh when seated side-by-side, holding hands while walking down the street, your arm around the shoulders on the sofa, gives your partner a warm feeling and conveys the love and affection you feel. The littlest touch can be as important, even if not more important than the longest night of sexual intimacy.

Exude your sex appeal and present a sexier you often to your partner. Put a spark back into your sexiness to show your lover that you need to feel the passion that you deserve. Giving day-to-day activities a sultry makeover will guarantee different fun things for you. Change your night dresses/gowns, bedroom beddings and curtains from time to time. Spicy lingerie, easy access clothes and sexy robes should be worn at home for a sex appeal. Sex does not have to start the minute the lights go off. If you feel sexy, your body is more apt to be open to sexual and intimate experiences. Married people should feel and think sexy, and they will enjoy sex more. Sex should be good exercise to lovers and married persons because it could help to burn calories, lower depression, and relax the body. Discover the sexy inner you by thinking about your right to pleasure. You might consider taking a sexy burlesque class and surprise your partner with an erotic striptease. You can also arrange a dinner party for friends as a casual get-together sizzle.

Tell your partner what you like most about them, what you admire, and what makes you proud. Building a romantic relationship is not just about the initial bonding. It is also about encouraging and supporting each others growth over the course of your lives. Share more with your partner more than you do with anyone else. There is a need for some personal space but give as much of yourself and your time to your partner. It is also true that sexiness has a way of sneaking up at the most improbable moments. Listen to what bothers your partner and offer whatever help; even if it is just sympathy. Make "alone times" a priority and commit one evening every week to be together. Give material tokens of your love to assure your partner that you are thinking of them.

Below are some tips to re-kindle the flames of love and romance among couples that are essential for a life-time marriage relationship:

1. Start dating again. Go out at least once a week. It does not have to be an expensive date-just something simple and affordable; taking a walk with your partner; going to the gym together, going to a movie, putting the kids to bed early, talking, tickling, and laughing together. A nice relaxing out door dinner for two would break the monotony of matrimonial life.

2. Restore the spark in your marriage. Try having soft background music in the living room and in the

bedroom at all times. Do not feel intimate only at bedtime, try touching, and cuddling as often as you can during the day, thus preparing for bed time. Before hurrying out for work in the morning give your partner a hug or 30 seconds kiss. Your partner responds with passion that would last for the day and will elicit usually a desire to see you come home early or reconnect with you at home. Say something funny to each other and have a good laugh to lighten the burdens of matrimony or the stress of paying bills or raising the kids.

3. Make yourself more attractive. Remember that the beautiful ones are not yet born, and that your partner is exposed everyday to the good things that the eyes can see. Buy new clothes, change pajamas and/or new sexy night gowns. Men should shave their beards and wear colognes that attracted their spouse during dating, and women should change constantly their make-ups, perfumes, and hairstyles. Both parties should try upgrading their looks and maintain the features that initially attracted you to each other. Changes you make in your appearance can precipitate changes in your spouse. In fact, try getting your spouse's attention as much as you can. It is ironic that

if you make yourself more attractive, your spouse will often become more attractive to you.

4. Celebrate yourselves. At festivities and birthdays, do something affordable, and exciting as a couple. Let your spouse know that he or she is worthy to be celebrated and write an appreciative note or buy cards, simple gifts to commemorate such occasions. Give yourselves surprises and treats as can be accommodated within the family budget.

5. Help yourselves. Sweet interaction within the home should be sustained with simple things as picking up your spouse's underwear from the floor, giving a free back rub, preparing meals, helping with domestic chores, serving your partner a drink on bed, a meal, etc. These little things build intimacy and closeness and give the marriage the desired fragrance and sparkle.

6. Communicate your desires to your spouse. Do so in non-threatening, judgmental ways. Remember that your spouse should be your best friend. Talk over the small things that bother you, and make yourself clear in the things you want. Be open to conversation and discus careers and goals with your partner as

much as you can so that problems can be fixed early. Discus sexual relations as often as you can to enhance romance, intimacy and the satisfaction of a lifetime.

13

Sexual Dysfunction In Men And Women

Negative sex enhancers

Sexual dysfunction is any aspect of sexual response that causes you or your partner dissatisfaction or distress. Low libido, medications, aging, vaginal dryness, erectile incompetence, physical, and mental health conditions can cause sexual dysfunction, emotional distance, and loss of intimacy. These conditions should not impair someone's love life, intimacy, and romance because an enjoyable and satisfying sex life is possible.

There should be a willingness to step out of your comfort zone to discover what really turns you on. Discuss your fantasies as well as frustration in love making with your partner. The responsibility is on you to re-discover the romance and passion in your relationship. Romance is about "whatever turns you on." Mastering the art of foreplay is required for a healthy sex life with your partner to avoid monotony and a drab sex life. Massage, eye contact, delicate arousals, hugs, and orgasms all increase love hormones. Intimacy is pleasurable, and effort should be made to enhance it because it is the foundation of most successful unions.

Couples should make sure to keep their date nights exciting and spontaneous — and their sex lives will respond in turn. Couples should get out of the axis of parent, and put chemistry back into their relationship as it was in the beginning. Efforts should be made continuously to reconcile the erotic and the domestic; so that lovemaking does not become boring and nightmarish. Love making should be an event to look forward to with your partner. Break out of your routine if it feels like the spark is fizzling.

About 40% of all women complain of low sex drive at some point in their lives. Many women have never experienced an orgasm in their lives. Female sexual desire directly correlates with physical, emotional, and psychological factors like illnesses, menopause, and relationship status. It is normal for female sex drive to drop or increase over time. Depression, exhaustion, and stress can drain libido, and diminish sexual interest. A realization of the health benefits of the sperm and the male semen perhaps will stir women's continual appetite for sex. Sperm and the seminal fluid contain more than 50 chemicals. These include serotonin which is an anti-depressant and oxytocin, which is a mood enhancing chemical the "love hormone" that has also been linked to orgasm and anxiety reduction.

Women who are regularly exposed to semen have fewer episodes of depression for the known fact that vaginal exposure to semen elevated women's mood. The walls of the vagina are highly absorptive, and it is easy for the feel-good elements to find their way in it. The caution is that this makes sexually transmitted diseases much riskier. An unwanted pregnancy and sexually transmitted diseases would offset any advantageous psychological effects of semen. Menopausal women no longer at risk at becoming pregnant, and with partners free of STDs might have to smile for the enormous health gains of having sex regularly.

Medications that treat depression and anxiety have the effect of killing sex drive. Genital tract and breast surgeries can also affect body function and desire for sex. Hormonal imbalance can put a damper on a woman's sex drive like hormone changes during pregnancy, after child birth, and the transition to menopause. Painful intercourse or inability to attain orgasm can make women avoid sex altogether. Men should avoid being in a hurry, and give their women quality romance for mutual pleasure. Excessive drinking can cause reduced blood flow causing vaginal secretions to dry up. Taking care of responsibilities, managing family, and career could take the smile off the face of the woman and affect the mood for sex.

There is also a case of low libido for women who have undergone circumcision or female genital mutilation. Female circumcision is the partial or total cutting away of the external female genitalia. During the operation, all or part of the clitoris or labia are removed, and this can hinder sexual arousals in women; making the affected women to require more foreplay before sexual intercourse. These surgical procedures have no health benefits for girls and women. It is internationally recognized as a violation of the human rights of girls and women. It reflects deep rooted inequality between the sexes, and constitutes an extreme of discrimination against women.

Many women have a problem with their libido or have completely lost their interest in sex. Loss of interest in sex is one of the most common female sexual problems. For some of these women to enjoy sex, they need vaginal lubrication and relaxed vaginal muscles. Vaginal dryness is a sign of loss of libido, and such women should have vaginal lubrication, sexual sensation, and interest in sex to be exciting partners. Women who want to enhance their libido can use topical creams to stimulate blood flow, alleviate vaginal dryness, and increase sexual response. Women should find pleasure in having sex regularly in their marriages because the walls of a woman's vagina absorb vital nutrients inherent in the male sperm. Women could lounge in a bubble bath with that perfume that has that soft, sensual smell to feel sexy all over again.

More than 45% of men make use of sex performance enhancers and energy boosting drugs. Sex enhancing drugs can treat erectile dysfunction but may have potentially serious side effects in some men. The desire to have multiple orgasms and issues of penal incompetence are some of the reasons men use sex enhancing drugs. More than 85% of men have more than one round of sex and have a high energy performance. Consequently, there could be an over-use of the penal tissues as a result of the drugs. The penis is a muscle and just like any muscle in the body can be overused, the penis can also be overused.

Sex enhancing drugs are capable of causing earth-quaking orgasms. There is the possibility of getting addicted to the drugs as well as health implications. Medical approval and supervision should be sought before involvement with sex enhancers to avoid health problems. Some of the health implications are prolonged painful erection, urinary incontinence, high blood pressure, anemia, arthritis, muscle pain, depression, seizure, asthma, sinusitis, vomiting, congestive heart disease, sudden death, bleeding within the brain and blood vessel problems; dry mouth are some of the many side effects of sex enhancing drugs. Other side effects are fainting, migraines, allergic reactions, back pain, rashes, joint pain, flu, dizziness, urinary tract disease, indigestion, face flushing, headaches, diarrhea, nasal congestion, bleeding in the lungs, loss of memory, gout, anxiety, sleep problems, heart attack, stroke, vision and hearing loss. Sex enhancers are slow killers, therefore, natural techniques are preferred. Penal erection is a process often initiated as a result of sexual arousal, when signals are transmitted from the brain to the nerves of the penis. Penal or erectile incompetence is the inability to achieve or maintain an erection satisfactory for sexual intercourse. Medical conditions, hormonal deficiencies or drug side effects are among the causes of erectile dysfunction. Prescription medication can cause sexual desire to fizzle. Sometimes, some men feel it is a challenge to their masculinity, and they start to withdraw from physical contact with their partners or maintain brooding silence.

Alternative treatments that will not have these negative effects should be considered. Personality disorders, stress, substance abuse, panic and anxiety disorders are among the psychological causes of penal incompetence. Aging and smoking could cause erectile dysfunction as well. Surgery of the prostrate, bladder, colon are also likely causes. Constant sex can cause over-usage and damage of the penis.

Renewed potency is possible, and it can avert depression or painful memories. Psychotherapy, drug therapy, vacuum devices, or surgery are used to treat erectile dysfunction. Penal implants can be fitted surgically to aid erection while aerobic exercise is an effective treatment for erectile dysfunction. Aerobic exercise can help keep the heart pumping and the blood flowing. Exercise generally could increase stamina and self-esteem. Conversation, partner cooperation, and high romantic spirit are antidotes of erectile incompetence. Humor and laughter can restore intimacy and reassure your partner that all is well. Partners should be supportive and sexy to propel sexual excitements at these brooding moments. Even holding hands and walking somewhere with lots of pretty lights can ignite lover's romantic feelings toward each other, and there will be raging hormones again.

When the passion candle is burning a little bit low, couples begin to feel "low." To rev up libido for love making, eat a diet low in fats and sugars with high nutrition and fiber foods; along with whole grain and low fat dairy products. Be musical because music is the food for the soul, and can kindle the romantic spirit. Try good healthy sleep to give your body the chance to refresh and recuperate from constant sex. Avoid alcohol and tobacco because they can harm sexual function. Be honest to your partner about your concerns and what satisfies you, however, discus concerns, worries, and more negative issues outside the bedroom.

The brain is an important sexual organ through which electrical signals discharge or reciprocate feelings. It is, therefore, necessary to think about your desires and sexual fantasies more often. Cuddle, hug, kiss, and hold hands with your partner if you are not in the mood for sex. During love making, experiment with touching your partner in new ways that could improve your sexual technique. Be inventive by spicing your bedroom, leaving love notes, plan an erotic getaway, try making love at different times of the day and at different locations to add color and excitement to your relationship.

Restore the element of drama and romance into a stale relationship by reading your partner a love poem or doing eyes' dancing to attract your partner. Eye's dancing is a non-verbal form of communication. Partners should also use sensuous body language to attract their partners. Even bees have been known to dance to attract their mates.

Take small sips of red wine daily. Red wine is parked with nutrients that protect the body against the effects of stress and aging. Eat well to replenish lost energy and add ginger and spicy meals to stir up the love hormones. Show respect always and use passionate words to caress your partner as often as you can. Passionate words break down the walls of resistance and bring out the best of emotions. It is not good to use your partner for "sexual release" only for this will make sex a duty routine and uninteresting.

Lovers should take a warm bath together in their Jacuzzi bath tub as a "romantic extra" to re-kindle the flame again. Romance should not be one-sided; there should be participation of both partners for more elating moments. Exciting sceneries with a partner, choice music, and ecstatic experiences are panacea and possible ways to get erection naturally. Sexual relationship is sharing most intimate behavior, and couples should get into bedroom adventures to discover what thrills their partner.

Loving is a range of human emotions. It is an intense interpersonal attraction that should excite partners even in difficult circumstances or erectile incompetence. Love refers to the passionate desire and intimacy of romantic love. Real love flows from the deep springs of the heart. It is an emotion of strong affection and personal attachment. Partners should be able to understand the bodies of their partners. Know what tickles your partner, and how to get him or her high. This helps to prevent dependency or usage of sex enhancing drugs. Just observing the body of your partner could be arousing because love is the most baffling of human emotions.

In romantic love relationships, romance implies the expression of one's emotional desire to connect with another person. Its maximum flavor needs to be "stirred up." It is an intense affection or warm feeling for another; like being hit by Cupid's arrows. Falling in love erupts like an earthquake and that should stimulate the erectile tissues sufficiently to gain or sustain an erection. Romance is a frenzy of wild and intoxicating feeling. Romance is an electrifying sensation that can send positive vibrations through the spine of your partner and awaken desire and turgidity. It is the pleasurable feeling of excitement, and mystery associated with love. Commitment, affection, and devotion are elements of a passionate relationship. Romance also recaptures the essence of what it is like to be in true love.

Attraction toward the opposite sex is something genetically ingrained in man because it is crucial in the continuation of the human specie. The primal instinct dictates sexual behavior and attracts the opposite sex. Hormones play a lot of role in the early stages of romantic relationships, which cause people to be giddy and overexcited. During romance, the body releases hormones called "pleasure chemicals." The love hormone, oxytocin increases intimacy, and bonding during romantic relationships. It is released in the body during hugging and intimate touch and plays a strong role in romance.

Massage, eye contacts, hugs, orgasms all increase love hormones. Orgasm is the ultimate human sexual pleasure. Nurturing this love hormone is one of the best ways to sustain romantic relationships for a life time. High levels of estrogens in persons involved in a passionate romance may cause excitability and sleeplessness. These hormones traverse the blood brain barrier and activate neurological synapses with electrifying results. Sudden piquant surprises could tickle your partner's fancy, and it is a great stimulation that rekindles the embers of love and love making.

A case in point was Sharon. She noticed that Harry her husband of 13 years was losing erectile turgidity. He was getting moody and depressed because he could no longer sustain an erection. They considered the option of using drug enhancers to keep up with their sex lives as a couple, the destructive effects notwithstanding. They are a young couple and that made her to go the extra mile to do bedroom makeovers, including cool lights and cool music. Sharon became svelte; so that her hussy will reminiscent on her youthfulness again. She placed herself on a bland diet to reinvent herself for that sexy and sensual look. She glamorized herself with a new wardrobe of clothes, night gowns, easy access clothes, and some unique fragrances.

At bedtime, she would wear sexy lingerie and robes. She also had preferences for bright color outfits. Red is an arousing color that gets people's blood pumping, and she leveraged on such colors for romantic effects. Attraction causes the blood to flow to the pleasure driven area of the brain, leading to a fixation with the person involved. This could help the situation as she presents a sweeter looking Sharon to Harry, her husband of 13 years.

Sharon began to look luscious and adorable. She remembered that her husband got randy on bluesy music easily during their dating sprees and courtship days. She also remembered that he felt good sitting under dimly lit chandeliers in cozy environments clicking on the wine glasses as they celebrate their wedding anniversaries. Harry popped the question and slipped the engagement ring on her fingers in one of those romantic settings. Sharon decided to re-visit the scenarios for a possible pep in their relationship. At bedtime, she would have bluesy addictive tunes vibrate the walls of their bedroom, and this act re-established their romantic evenings. Music choices did the talking for them, and it was an ecstatic world again for the two love birds.

It was Harry's 35th birthday, and she planned a surprise. Harry came home from work at twilight, and expected just a good dinner to celebrate the occasion. Sharon had put the kids to bed early; so that she can be all his for the asking. There were candles leading to their bedroom and candles that outlined their bed. The bed was set like a picnic with placemats. In deed, any arousing activity can trigger feelings of romance as a side effect. Harry was bewildered with the romantic welcome, and he was treated to a delightful dinner. To pep him up for a sexual response for his birthday, Sharon had taken a sexy burlesque class and surprised her husband with an erotic striptease.

As Sharon and Harry cuddled with elation, a frenzy of hormones and neurochemical activity occurred. Oxytocin promotes bonding between a man and a woman through touch. Hand holding, cuddling, snuggling, hugging or even being in the proximity of a lover can cause the release of oxytocin. By increasing desire and arousal, there is also enhanced bonding between the partners. Couples entering into the state of love tend to be "floating" almost immune from the worries of the world. It is a fact that when a woman really likes her guy, her libido hits through the roof.

With a little sip of Champagne for a birthday toast, their evening was set for the most ecstatic love making they have ever had. They turned the lights low and drifted into an utopian realm; almost immune from the worries of the world. They were humming along in harmony as a passionate pair, resolved to give themselves sizzling moments routinely.

Sizzling 40 Years

My spouse is altogether lovely;
Her breasts are like twin grapes

L iz and Denny's story is a ravishing and blissful
matrimonial experience transfused with the memories
of their first date. It is a union embellished with constant
demonstrations of love, soaring on the wings of adoration
and the fidelity of a twosome. It is an ideal marriage,
standing astride in a world barraged with divorce, spousal
battery, and spousal homicide. This is a tantalizer for
all married persons, and those who wish to be married.

Marriages can indeed bloom and blossom for a life time.

It was at a gala night in Brooklyn New York, that I met Liz for the first time. In dazzling apparel, Liz arrived with an overwhelming confidence. Her eyes glittered with bold shades and darkly lined eyes. Liz, with her captivating eye lashes, a glowing skin and sizzling smiles, was very much distinguished amidst the august audience. She was wearing a fabulous red dress with diamante studs that had a giant cascade of frills slashed below the waist. Red is an arousing color that gets people's blood pumping. She looked stunning with a stoic elegance and poise, and she was wearing a sleek, sexy and straight hairstyle.

As Liz settled into a chair by my side with a mirthful smile, I responded to her infectious smile with complimentary remarks. She was bubbling with so much youthfulness as she responded "I will be 60 in October and looking and feeling youthful keep me from wrinkles and aging." We became conversational and she gave me insights into her happy life and marriage. Apparently, Denny her husband is her lover and best friend. Liz is profuse about Denny, and talks about him at every opportunity. The glitz and glamour surrounding Liz and the spontaneous smiles she emits intermittently is perhaps usual with people who are contented and having a great deal of romantic moments.

Liz has been married to Denny for 40 years. Their sizzling love for each other was sustained on the wings of love, respect, and romance. I inquired about the secret of their entrancing love for each other and Liz responded "it's been 40 years of marriage, and whenever Denny makes love to me, I hit orgasm many times, and my toes curl in ecstatic delight with each experience. Each experience is as intoxicating as it was in the beginning." Surely, Liz and Denny live in tranquil emotions; despite matrimonial tides and upheavals. This is because they decided to cling to the passions of yesterday, and enhance the romantic glitz of the present until death do them part. They are poised to make true their marital vows, and refresh their love with a new fragrance each passing day.

Couples should make love and not war. Married persons should hold onto their marital vows and nourish them with as much passion as they can muster each minute and each day. When love is not tended, it withers and dies perhaps forever. Couples should develop a romantic spirit to continually re-kindle libido when it is waning. Additionally, people who enjoy orgasm many times in their lives could add extra eight to ten years to their life span. Such people also are more likely to look younger than their real age as is the case with Liz.

A romantic bed is a happy bed to visit each night, and couples should look forward to being on bed for romantic togetherness. The grass is not always greener on the other side, and perhaps you have your soul mate in your hands if you will learn to appreciate what you have. Infidelity and the lustful desires for sexual variety is a cankerworm that eats deeply into the marriage fabric.

Matrimonial relationships do not have blood ties. The nexus is the romantic sentiments that earlier defined the choice of a spouse. Your spouse is your life, and you should give yourself in every special way to your spouse daily. This will constantly add color to relationships, and keep the couples magnetized to each other in mystifying ardor. It will also reduce incidences of conflict, separation and divorce. Health gains and longevity of life will also come into the equation.

Honey is sweet and every one craves for it. When you give your heart to your sweetheart, the best of you comes in full bloom, and you can sustain a high level libido that enhances desire and thrilling moments. This could minimize issues of frigidity and domestic violence. Liz has shut the doors of divorce and squabbles, and she unfolded her daily recipe for this. At this point, I drifted into wonderland in anticipation of the prescriptive recipe of a loving and enduring marriage.

Passionate love usually has a life span of about 30 months. Liz and Denny's experience seem to have faulted this research finding. Liz and Denny in a reciprocating love are drenched in passionate love with each other spanning an impressive 40 years. They seem poised to keep swimming in the ocean of love as they pitch their tent in the world of romance.

Shortly, her husband Denny joined us at table, and it became a table of three. Liz introduced Denny who arrived with an egotistic confidence. He was wearing a Gucci Signoria tuxedo, which he paired with patent leather shoes. It was a pleasant evening at the gala night, and the couple invited me for dinner at their Brooklyn home in a forth night.

I kept having flashbacks of the charming couple until I sat at dinner in their exquisitely furnished home for the dinner date two weeks later. It was a refreshing time, and we sat in the gardens with exotic plants and flowers sipping red wine. Red wine is parked with nutrients that protect the body against the effects of aging, thereby, helping keep the body youthful. It was also a buffet style dinner that we had afterwards. I inquired further about their bubbling relationship "do you get bored sometimes, and wish that he was gone on business trips?" Liz responded "it has been a blissful 40 years being married to Denny. I still feel the same as on our wedding day, when we shared the marriage vows before a delightful audience. I was 17, and Denny was 19 when we went on our first date, and he still accords me all the curtsies as it was in the beginning. Whenever he is on a business trip, I can't wait to have him back home, and when we are on bed, I can't wait for that moment. He thrills me like new wine each time he reaches out for that warm and delightful curdle."

Surprised at her response, I interjected "how do you sustain such passionate intimacy for a period of 40 years?" Responding she said "fundamentally, Denny and I are friends, and we vibrate on the same social strata, and we have similar interests. I eat skimpy meals, and work at looking good each day of the 40 years to keep my weight within manageable limits for his arms. That makes him feel that it is the same as it was in the very beginning. I never forget the adage that the beautiful ones are not yet born, and that there are other trendy females out there who could get his attention. Denny has a teeming population of females at his workplace, and that keeps me on my toes looking my best.

Denny interjected that they make occasional visits to the beach, and have get-a-away nights to watch a galaxy of theatrical performers and opera stars. This allows them to still have a feel of the things they enjoyed doing 40 years ago. In making sure that the "honey" does not leave the "moon", they have affordable vacations to re-live the ecstatic moments of the past. Liz interjected jocularly "we keep our youthfulness with new trends and activities that feel invigorating. To get and keep his attention, I wear captivating make ups, different hair styles, maintaining also a sizzling wardrobe so as to look charmingly youthful for him –just like the Liz he met 40 years ago. I join him for his sports as often as I can, and I get prepared for bedtime with sexy night gowns and a mild talcum powder for that refreshing feel and sizzling moment."

Denny in turn reciprocates with new things that bring excitement. He comes home with surprise gifts and flowers from time to time, while Liz reciprocates with men's stuff. He wears cute haircuts and entrancing perfumes for men that entice Liz. They give themselves romantic hugs or smacks during the day even when they are keeping up with tight business schedules. These seducing initiatives give their union of 40 years a romantic rhythm that prepares them for midnight delights. they have worked hard to keep themselves constantly in their colorful world.

The refreshing and fascinating evening with the two love birds, gave me a peep into their blissful world, a world where they dwell in inspiring awe of each other's fragrance, a real-world of a real twosome, two love birds bewildered in enthusiastic ardor. At this point, I congratulated Liz and Denny for a sizzling 40 years together, exchanged business cards, and thanked them profusely for sharing the evening with me.

15

Pep Talk

Your lips drop as the honeycomb

You can look cute even if you don't let too much of your "goods" hang out. Girls should not showcase all their body assets. This could give the wrong impression and could make people uncomfortable, thereby, scaring the best guys away.

* Sometimes, guys want these "goods" for their eyes only.

* Sex means two different things to men and women. A male needs sexual release upper and foremost. This is just plain raw sex, and he doesn't care where it comes from. His body is pouring chemicals to his brain to cause a driving need for sexual release.

* It is not good to use your partner for "sexual release" only; for this will make sex a duty routine and uninteresting. Give your partner affection and a delightful sexual advance.

* Women enjoy reciprocity in feelings, and not just receptacles for a man's "release."

* Men should pep up the woman's best feelings at all times to get the best of her sexual responses.

* Sex should be introduced in the midst of heightened romantic pleasures when both partners (not only one) are ready for the sexual experience.

* Men hurry to gain penetration, and they forget that firstly, the woman's body should be mesmerized.

* Love making is not a hurried affair. It is a time to spend quality time with your sweet heart for thrilling moments.

*   Women are sweetly disposed to romance, tender caresses, treats, surprises, and outward demonstrations of love in public or in private, and all these prepare women for satisfactory sexual performance.

*   Sex enhancing drugs are capable of causing earth-quaking orgasms, which could have gross health implications. Rejuvenate your sexual performance with sweet music tunes and enchanting atmosphere. Get naturally sexy, and have a thrilling partner instead of using sex enhancing drugs.

*   If you are a sex maniac, or if you have a sex addiction, try to bridle your desire so that you do not exhaust your partner, and turn sex into a nightmare.

*   Look into the eyes of your special someone often, for the eyes are the window to the soul.

*   A courtship begins when a man whispers sweet nothings, and ends when he says nothing sweet.

*   A happy wife is a happy life; make your wife happy!

*   Do not allow the spark to leave your marriage, and don't fall out of love at the same time with your partner, someone got to sustain it.

* Girls, have a confident poise always, and avoid clinging desperately to your guy because a man will choose an unavailable average girl to a clingy beauty.

* Men like cute-butt jeans

* Groom yourself and try looking good for your partner always. Keeping your weight in check is simple courtesy to your partner.

* Don't be selfish; take time to give your partner some romance to avoid frigidity and infidelity.

* High-quality men are drawn to ambitious women. If a guy is intimidated by you, he doesn't deserve you.

* Girls, wear maxi-dresses with some slit to show a little bit of skin for a more attractive you.

* Girls, do not put your guy under pressure of any sort; no guy wants a desperate woman.

* If you treat your girl right, she will always be ready for you.

* Make dazzling impressions on your first date in the first few seconds; so that your date can form great opinions of you. This will guarantee a retake. On

first dates, men should not pry or ask questions that will make a girl squirm. Focus on keeping her comfortable, and smile most often asking about her interests and passions.

* To make a good impression on your first date, ax the word "ex" from your conversation. The word "ex" is too loaded. Try to avoid resurrecting your "baggage" too early.

* Avoid ordering whiskeys and vodkas on your first date; so that you do not give the wrong impressions, and more especially so that you remain sane through the date.

* For married females only – wear easy access and colorful nightgowns at bedtime. Men are visual creatures, and they are attracted to the good things they see.

* Couples should give themselves occasional breaks from sexual intercourse; so as to allow their bodies rest and recuperate from sexual activity.

* Couples should not have a timetable to have sex, and they should not have sex only at a particular time and at a particular place.

* Give your bedrooms a romantic décor on Valentine Days, Birthdays, and other festivity periods. The bedroom may just be the most important room in your home because the magic happens there.

* Girls should fix their guy's collar when he is dressed for work or a meeting or an outing. There is something so divine about an unexpected, casual, sweet touch. It makes guys feel all warm and happy.

* Men and women both judge books by their covers, especially on first dates; so make an effort in your appearance. Don't be tardy on your first date and do not keep your date waiting. If your date invites his buddies along with you for the movies, parties or dinner, it is likely to be a downward relationship spiral. It is no longer a date but a group thing. If he just scans the venue instead of focusing on you, he is getting ready to move on his way out of the relationship.

* Open communication can prevent a downward relationship spiral.

* A person who is cheating suddenly wants to look better. When a guy starts working out, begins to have an extreme makeover, and suddenly buys new clothes,

he is looking to impress other women. When your man starts taking better care of himself, he may well be contemplating replacing you.

* Watch out if your guy becomes suddenly critical and judgmental. A girl deserves to be worshipped, not tortured by a guy and when he begins to jump down your throat for no reason, you have become the "spinach" in his bowl that he doesn't want anymore. Love is supposed to be fun.

* Watch out when he starts canceling your dates because he is crazy busy at work and when he does not discuss plans with you. Take note when he reduces his calls, and his car is no more in the drive-way or he no longer knocks on the door. These are "tells," spelling out his time-to-get-outta-here intentions and that he is getting ready to break free.

* Couples should avoid conflicting schedules; so that they will have ample time to connect romantically. They can hire a babysitter sometimes, so as to enjoy a candle light dinner away from home.

www.ingramcontent.com/pod-product-compliance
Lightning Source LLC
Chambersburg PA
CBHW050727030426
42336CB00012B/1442